Devil, PLEASE

REVISED AND EXPANDED

I AM STILL NOT OFFENDED

AYANNA LYNNAY

Devil Please I am Still Not Offended

© December 2024

By Ayanna Lynnay

Published in the United States of America by

ChosenButterflyPublishing LLC

www.ChosenButterflyPublishing.com

ISBN: 978-1-945377-43-3
Revised Edition Printing
Printed in the United States of America
December 2024

To those I have offended, forgive me; and to those who have offended me, I forgive you.

Table of Contents

Introduction

Offense—it's something we've all faced. A careless word, a misunderstood gesture, or a betrayal from someone we trusted. It stings, doesn't it? Offense has a unique ability to burrow deep into our hearts, causing wounds that linger far beyond the initial event. And if we're not careful, those wounds can grow, fester, and harden into bitterness and resentment, robbing us of the joy and peace God intends for our lives. But what if I told you that you don't have to live that way? What if you could rise above the traps of offense and step into a life of freedom, healing, and victory?

This isn't just another book about forgiveness or conflict resolution—this is a journey of transformation. Offense isn't merely an emotional reaction or a bad day. It's a weapon the enemy uses to derail your destiny, distract you from God's purpose, and destroy relationships that could have been sources of blessing. Satan knows the power of offense because he's been using it since the beginning of time. But here's the good news: the Lord has equipped you with the tools to not only withstand the enemy's schemes but to grow and flourish in the midst of them.

In these pages, we'll explore what it truly means to overcome the spirit of offense. You'll learn how to recognize offense for what it is—a spiritual attack—and how to respond in a way that glorifies God and strengthens you. This isn't about denying your feelings or pretending offenses don't hurt; it's about choosing to see them through God's eyes, trusting His process, and walking in obedience to His Word. With biblical principles, personal testimonies, and practical tools, this book will empower you to live unoffended, not by your strength but by God's.

We'll delve into some tough questions: Why does offense hurt so much? How do you forgive someone who isn't sorry? How can offense be a stepping stone rather than a stumbling block? Through the lives of biblical figures like Joseph, Jesus, and others, we'll uncover how God can take the most painful offenses and turn them into powerful testimonies of His grace and faithfulness.

But this isn't just about you. When you overcome offense, you're not only setting yourself free—you're creating space for others to see God's love in action. Your victory over offense will heal relationships, restore hope, and even open doors for ministry. Imagine becoming so unoffendable that the enemy's schemes no longer have power over you. Picture yourself walking in a peace so profound that it confounds those who try to hurt you. Envision a life where God's purpose shines so brightly through you that it transforms the people and situations around you.

This journey won't always be easy. There will be moments when you'll feel justified in your hurt, tempted to hold on to your pain. But I promise you, the freedom waiting on the other side is worth every moment of struggle. As someone who's faced deep hurts and betrayals, I can testify that God's healing power is real and transformative. I've learned to say, "Devil, please—I am still not offended!" and mean it with every fiber of my being. That same victory is available to you.

So, if you're tired of letting offense dictate your emotions, relationships, and decisions, I invite you to embark on this journey. Together, we'll uncover how to turn offense into opportunities for growth, strength, and ministry. It's time to take back your peace, reclaim your joy, and walk in the authority God has given you.

Are you ready to rise above? Let's step into a life where offense no longer has a say in who you are or where you're going. A life where God's purpose and power reign supreme. The choice is yours. Let's begin.

Devil Please, I Am Still Not Offended

The piercing knife in my back seemed to go straight through my heart.

"Oh no, not again."

The familiar feelings of betrayal, hurt, and emotional abuse surged all at once. Why did it seem like the people I loved, respected, and admired were the ones causing the deepest wounds to my heart, mind, and spirit?

What did I do to deserve this? Ever since I accepted Christ, I've made it my mission to walk in unconditional love. I've strived to be a blessing, supporting others every chance I got. And yet, this was my reward?

"Father, are you serious?" The ache of hurt and betrayal twisted, threatening to turn into anger and bitterness.

My mind raced with thoughts I didn't want to entertain:

- "How dare they treat me like this?"
- "I don't have to put up with this!"
- "That's it—I'm leaving this church."

In that storm of emotions, I heard the Holy Spirit speak: **"No, you are going to stay."**

"Stay? Father, is that You?"

This had to be a joke. My mind was playing tricks on me. Surely, the devil wanted me to stay so he could keep using people to emotionally harm me and stunt my spiritual growth. Why would God want me to remain in a place where leadership caused so much pain?

The Holy Spirit responded, **"I am going to teach you how to stand and be an overcomer. I will show you how to recognize and overcome a spirit that is destroying churches, families, and relationships of all kinds."**

This spirit's name is OFFENSE, and it is a master of disguise.

The Anatomy of Offense

Offense doesn't walk into your life with a name tag that says, "I'm here to ruin you." No, offense is cunning and subtle, often camouflaged as righteous indignation, justified anger, or even well-meaning advice. It sneaks into your heart, sowing seeds of discord, resentment, and division.

I began to realize that offense was like a parasite. Once it takes root, it feeds on your emotions, thoughts, and even your relationships. It twists perspectives, magnifies misunderstandings, and distorts reality.

The Holy Spirit started revealing moments in my life where offense had stolen my peace, disrupted my joy, and hindered my ability to love unconditionally.

I thought about the time I felt overlooked for a promotion at work. Instead of being happy for my colleague, I let bitterness fester. Or the time a family member said something harsh during a holiday gathering. Rather than seeking to understand, I chose to stew in hurt.

The Lord showed me that offense is a choice. While we cannot control what people say or do to us, we can control how we respond. That realization was both liberating and convicting.

The Hard Truth

Choosing not to be offended doesn't mean ignoring the hurt or pretending it didn't happen. It doesn't mean letting people walk all over you. It means acknowledging the hurt but refusing to let it control you. It means choosing forgiveness even when you feel the other person doesn't deserve it.

I wrestled with this concept. "Lord, how can I forgive when they haven't even apologized?"

His response? **"Forgiveness is not about them; it's about freeing you."**

Forgiveness isn't excusing what happened—it's releasing the power it holds over you. It's giving God the permission to heal your heart while He deals with the other person in His time and His way.

Ten Years Later

When I first published this book in 2014, I had no idea how much my life would change in the years to come. Now, more than a decade later, I feel the Lord prompting me to revisit it, refine it, and share it again—this time with new insights and an accompanying course. That's exactly what I'm doing.

It's amazing; I haven't read through this manuscript in years, yet I can still vividly recall every situation—the emotions I experienced, the lessons I learned, and the way it all shaped me into who I am today. Though it was painful at the time, I am deeply grateful for every experience and the growth it brought into my life.

When I first wrote *Devil, Please I Am Not Offended*, I tiptoed around certain truths. This time, I'm offering fresh perspectives and deeper understanding, shedding light on just how sneaky and destructive offense can be. My prayer is that these revisions will help you break free from anything holding you back and empower you to walk in greater freedom and grace.

I also want to be honest about how tough it is to overcome. Forgiveness and choosing not to take offense aren't as easy as some make it seem. But it is possible. And the rewards for choosing forgiveness far outweigh the fleeting satisfaction of holding onto a grudge.

Even now, I'm still learning. Sometimes, I still struggle with offense. But looking back over the past ten years, I can boldly declare again: **Devil, Please I Am Still Not Offended.**

The Journey Ahead

This book isn't just about avoiding offense—it's about transforming how you see it. Offense doesn't have to be a stumbling block; it can be a stepping stone. Every offense is an opportunity to grow in grace, love, and spiritual maturity.

Let me leave you with this thought: Offense is inevitable, but bitterness is optional.

Jesus said, **"Offenses will certainly come, but woe to the one they come through!"** (Luke 17:1, CSB).

This verse reminds me that while we can't control when offense comes, we can control whether it stays. Let's choose freedom over frustration, love over resentment, and growth over grudges.

This is your moment to stand, overcome, and declare with boldness: **"Devil, please—I am STILL not offended!"**

It's Time to Grow Up

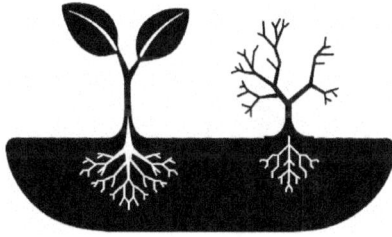

True spiritual maturity has little to do with your chronological age or how long ago you accepted Jesus as your personal Savior. Rather, it relates to the condition of your spiritual heart and your growth since accepting Jesus not just as your Savior, but as your Lord—meaning He is in control of your life, and you are following His lead. It's astonishing how many people accept Jesus as their Savior but progress no further. While they may not say it aloud, their lives and lifestyles express the sentiment: "Yes, Jesus, I accept You died for my sins so I won't have to go to hell, but I want to continue living my life as before. I want to live for me, even though You died so I could live for You."

This might sound absurd, but evidence abounds in churches everywhere. Visit any congregation and observe how many church-goers, including those who claim to have "been saved all their life," behave worse than new Christians. Some of these long-standing saints demonstrate the poorest examples of Christianity imaginable. They gossip, display mean-spiritedness, pass judgment, backbite, and might metaphorically remove your head for sitting in "their" seat. They parade around speaking in tongues but refuse to speak to fellow congregants in English. They act as if they have "arrived," expecting others to be grateful for their mere presence, demanding to be greeted first, and showing no signs of being lovable, welcoming, or kind.

Their behavior outside church—at home, work, in the community, even at social gatherings—often proves even worse. If not for their self-proclaimed Christian status or church title, no one would suspect they follow Christ.

A Tale of Transformation

Consider Sally from the street who, one Sunday morning a few months ago, felt compelled to visit church. Though never particularly religious, something told her to accept a friend's invitation. She experienced emotions she'd never felt before, and before she knew it, she found herself at the altar, weeping and uttering surprising words: "I want to know You, Lord. I want my life to change. I've tried changing my life, but it doesn't work. Help me! I am ready to surrender my life to You."

Six months later, people no longer call her "Sally from the Streets" but instead "Sally, the Jesus Freak." Those close to her have witnessed tremendous growth in her relationship with the Lord. She associates with different people, engages in different activities, speaks differently, dresses differently, and emanates an undeniable glow. Even skeptics of "this Jesus religion" can witness God's transforming power at work in Sally's life.

Sally's transformation begins internally, with external changes reflecting genuine inner growth. Soon, people seek her prayers, church leaders recognize God's anointing upon her, and her pastor asks her to share words of encouragement with the congregation. Sally willingly serves wherever she can bring glory to God. Newcomers, drawn by her invitations, visit the church, curious about what has transformed her life. Not everyone appreciates these changes, but we'll address that later...

A Personal Testament

Though Sally is fictional, her story mirrors many real experiences, including my own. I transformed from a life of promiscuity, drinking, marijuana use, and more into something completely different. Surprisingly, I wasn't actively seeking the Lord; I simply found myself thinking, "There has to be more to life than this." Despite being in my mid-twenties, married with children, working as a nurse, earning good money, maintaining friendships, and traveling, I felt miserable. I battled depression and cycled on and off medication that seemed ineffective. Unknown to me, my thought about life's meaning represented my heart crying out to the Lord—and He answered.

One day, while smoking at a friend's house, she decided to play a church recording. Despite my reluctance, she played a T.D. Jakes conference, "Woman, Thou Art Loosed," featuring Dr. Rita Twiggs. Although my friend fell asleep, Dr. Twiggs's words pierced through my haze and spoke to my spirit. While I didn't fully comprehend everything she said, it felt like someone flipped a light switch inside me. I returned home transformed. After discussing my desire to give my life to Christ with Christian family members, I immediately began attending church. For the first time, my depression's dark cloud lifted. Though I didn't yet understand my purpose, I felt purposeful, knowing it involved developing a relationship with the Lord. My eager pursuit of God accelerated my spiritual growth, and soon He used me in ways that surprised many long-time church-goers. This wasn't about seeking attention; it was about being used by God, though not everyone—especially those saved longer than I—appreciated it.

Understanding Spiritual Growth

I share my salvation story briefly to emphasize this point: Spiritual growth isn't determined by chronological age. We cannot dismiss others (or ourselves) based on salvation length, nor assume someone should reach a certain spiritual level merely because they've been saved for an extended period. Spiritual growth connects deeply to our heart condition.

Matthew 13 presents a parable outlining four different heart conditions: wayside, stony, thorny, and good soil.

The Wayside Heart

Wayside hearts hear the word but fail to understand it and don't seek clarity. It resembles attending a Spanish-speaking church your entire life without understanding Spanish. The devil easily snatches away the word due to this lack of understanding, hindering spiritual maturity and growth.

Treatment for a wayside heart includes:

- Praying for guidance to a church where you can understand the word.

- Asking questions of pastors or leaders.

- Reading the Bible in an understandable translation.

While some advocate exclusively for the King James Version, choose a translation that helps you understand God's message. Consult your pastor about different Bible translations, explore them, and select one you comprehend. When I first attended church, much remained unclear, but I prayed for understanding. I asked the Lord for revelation and knowledge of His word, listened to online sermons, and read books as He led me. Don't let confusion lead to frustration and surrender. The enemy wants to keep your heart in the wayside condition to stunt your spiritual growth. Determine to keep pressing forward. You'll discover blessings in the persistence. Initially, I avoided much of the Old Testament due to its complexity. Now, I preach many messages from it. You can achieve this too!

The Stony Heart

A stony heart becomes excited during worship or preaching but forgets these moments of victory when troubles arise. Such individuals stop believing in God's ability and claim righteousness is "too hard." They backslide in their commitment and devotion to the Lord, potentially abandoning church altogether. They fail to recognize that God used that choir's victory song or that preacher's empowering message because He knew what trials they would face. The Lord provided all necessary ammunition to fight the good fight of faith and develop deep spiritual roots. Instead of using this arsenal against the devil for victory, they accept defeat, claiming, "I can't make it." Lack of deep spiritual roots results in spiritual immaturity.

Treatment for a stony heart requires perseverance despite feelings. Deep spiritual roots develop not in good times but in challenging ones. During storms, hold onto the Word you heard, the songs you sang, and remember previous deliverances. Like physical exercise builds muscles, spiritual muscles need resistance to grow stronger. Each challenge presents an opportunity to strengthen faith. Change what you can about your situation, then trust God with what you cannot.

The Thorny Heart

Thorny hearts hear and understand the word, witnessing God's promises materialize in their lives. However, they become distracted once these promises manifest. Life's worries and wealth's allure cloud their judgment and suffocate the planted Word. The very blessings they prayed for begin to supersede God in their lives. Their devotion shifts from the Source to the resource. They become so focused on maintaining God's blessings that they lose sight of Him.

For example, after receiving a prayed-for large house, they might work constantly, including Sundays, to afford the mortgage, missing church services. Or, after receiving a prayed-for job, they might prioritize work over their relationship with God. This distraction severely impedes spiritual growth.

Another example might be someone who prayed for business success. When success arrives, instead of using it to advance God's Kingdom, they might become consumed by success—focusing on expanding finances and influence until business activities and social status consume all time and energy, leaving little for spiritual matters.

Treatment for a thorny heart involves maintaining constant gratitude to God for His blessings. God doesn't bless us to drive us away from Him. Disconnecting from Him often leads to disconnection from those blessings. Remember, when God blesses us with something or someone, we need Him even more to sustain those blessings. God will uphold and preserve what He has ordained for our lives, provided we keep our faith in Him and prioritize Him above everything else.

The Good Heart

The final heart condition in Matthew 13 is the good heart. This heart understands, endures, and develops deep spiritual roots without getting distracted. These individuals may have extensive experience or have been touched so profoundly that they'll do whatever necessary to avoid returning to old ways. They desire transformation and yearn for the Lord's presence. Because they hunger and thirst for righteousness, the Lord fills them. They don't look down on others because they remain focused on Jesus, seeking wholeness. The good heart can exist in anyone—young or old, long-saved or recently converted. The good heart demonstrates complete devotion to Jesus. This condition must exist and persist for spiritual maturity to develop.

The Journey to Maturity

Understand that we never reach complete spiritual maturity or total knowledge. However, spiritual maturity has levels, and greater maturity brings greater responsibility. This explains why one person might attend church for ten years with their life remaining chaotic, while another person, after just a few years, walks in Holy Ghost power and receives its accompanying blessings. Again, spiritual maturity depends not on how long Jesus has been your Savior but on how long you've allowed Him to be your Lord.

These heart conditions can change based on circumstances. Therefore, throughout your spiritual journey, regularly assess your heart condition to determine your status and apply necessary remedies to overcome wayside, stony, or thorny conditions.

Why Heart Condition Matters

Why focus on spiritual heart conditions in a discussion about offenses? Because I believe heart condition determines maturity level, which influences our reaction to offenses. The Lord desires our growth and maturity in Him. If our hearts exist in any state other than good soil, the enemy can easily offend, hinder, and even prevent us from becoming who God says we are and obtaining what He promises.

Life requires mastering certain lessons to grow, similar to school's specific curricula and tests. After demonstrating mastery—not just occupying space—you advance to the next level, gaining additional benefits, authority, and responsibilities. This principle applies both naturally and spiritually. The Lord has more in store for us, but it comes with readiness rather than self-will. How do we know we're ready? By passing the test.

God promised the Israelites a land flowing with milk and honey, symbolizing abundance, prosperity, and blessings. They required testing, so God avoided the shortest route. What should have taken eleven days became forty years of wilderness wandering, traveling in circles, and ultimately dying without reaching God's promises. They failed to trust and obey God despite difficulties. Everyone except Joshua and Caleb possessed either wayside, stony, or thorny hearts.

I refuse to live circularly because I failed to learn necessary lessons or repeatedly failed tests. I aim to learn quickly, despite potential pain, to advance to the next level.

Some learned lessons I pray never to forget, not just for their blessings but because of the associated pain I never wish to repeat. Dealing with OFFENSE ranks among the most painful lessons. During the learning process, I couldn't comprehend why I experienced it. The pain hurt deeply. I had to pray against anger and bitterness taking root in my heart. I felt angry with God for allowing it and even angrier with those who offended me.

Today, my perspective has completely changed. I recognize how learning to handle offenses properly helped me GROW UP and mature spiritually. It also provided material for this book to assist others on their journey—further proof that the Lord truly works everything together for good!

Saints, don't get offended—get delivered! Few things challenge or reveal our spiritual heart condition like offenses. But we cannot remain offended. An immature Christian will always be an easily offended Christian. It's time to grow up, move beyond our thoughts and feelings, and become more effective and useful for the Kingdom of God.

Recap:

- Spiritual maturity is not determined by age or the length of time you've been saved but by the condition of your heart and your willingness to let Jesus lead every area of your life.

- The parable of the sower in Matthew 13 illustrates four types of heart conditions:
    - **Wayside hearts**: Lack understanding and are easily snatched away by the enemy.
    - **Stony hearts**: Receive the Word with joy but falter during trials due to shallow roots.
    - **Thorny hearts**: Allow life's worries and blessings to choke out spiritual growth.
    - **Good hearts**: Understand, endure, and prioritize God, producing lasting spiritual fruit.

- Spiritual growth is a continuous process of self-assessment and persistence, especially in the face of challenges like offense. Offenses are key tests of spiritual maturity, revealing the true condition of our hearts.

Reflection Questions:

1. Which of the four heart conditions—wayside, stony, thorny, or good—best reflects where you are right now in your spiritual journey?

_____

_____

_____

2. Are there offenses, distractions, or trials currently hindering your growth? How have you been responding to them?

_____

_____

_____

3. How can you cultivate a heart that remains open, enduring, and focused on God, no matter the circumstances?

_____

_____

_____

4. Think of a recent test of spiritual maturity you faced. What did it reveal about your growth? How can you apply what you've learned to future challenges?

_____

_____

_____

5. Are there areas of your life where Jesus is Savior but not yet Lord? What steps can you take to surrender those areas fully to Him?

_____

_____

_____

Action Steps:

- **Assess Your Heart Condition:** Take time this week to reflect on which heart condition describes you. Ask God to show you areas where you need growth and healing.

- **Nurture Spiritual Roots:** Commit to deepening your relationship with God through consistent prayer, Bible study, and fellowship with other believers.

- **Guard Against Distractions:** Identify potential "thorns" in your life—whether they're worries, blessings, or misplaced priorities—and take steps to refocus on God.

- **Forgive Offenses Quickly:** Choose to release offenses as soon as they arise. Pray for the strength to forgive and trust God to use those moments for your growth.

- **Seek Accountability:** Surround yourself with spiritually mature believers who can encourage and challenge you to grow in your faith.

- **Celebrate Growth:** Take note of small victories in your spiritual journey and thank God for the progress He's making in your life.

Spiritual growth requires intentionality and surrender. By addressing the condition of your heart, learning from your experiences, and remaining rooted in God's Word, you can mature in faith and be equipped to handle life's challenges—including offenses—with grace and resilience.

Let's commit to growing up in Christ, knowing that with every step of faith, He leads us closer to His purpose for our lives. Let's press forward, saints, because greater is truly ahead!

The Weapon Has Been Formed

"**N**o weapon that is formed against thee shall prosper; and every tongue that shall rise against thee in judgment thou shalt condemn. This is the heritage of the servants of the LORD, and their righteousness is of me, saith the LORD." Isaiah 54:17, KJV

I'm sure you've heard that scripture, and if you're like me, you may have proudly quoted the abbreviated version, "No weapon formed against me shall prosper," especially during times of warfare. Often, we recite scripture believing in its truth, yet sometimes we must pause and really think, "What does this really mean, and how can I apply this scripture to my life?"

If we're going to quote Isaiah 54:17 in relation to offense, then it's crucial to understand what the weapon is and what it is formed to do. Let's first examine the term "weapon." A weapon is anything used against an opponent in attack or defense. The presence of a weapon implies a serious intent; it's not merely symbolic but a clear indication of preparedness for battle. If one person has a weapon and another does not, nine times out of ten, we already know who will win the battle.

Why Is Recognition Important?

Because you must recognize that Satan is forming spiritual weapons to attack and defend against his adversaries. And who are his adversaries? We are! Those of us who have said, "Yes" to the Lord Jesus and "No" to Satan and his ways are now Satan's opponents.

Before coming to Christ, many of us were unwittingly playing for the enemy's team. We lived life on our own terms, doing what we wanted, when we wanted, without any consideration for what the Lord wanted for us. Sin and negative behaviors were almost second nature. Reflecting on our past, we can connect with what the psalmist expressed in Psalm 51:5, "Surely I was sinful at birth, sinful from the time my mother conceived me." From birth, we were on the devil's side, learning his ways, which centered around self-gratification and disobedience. However, we cannot enter Heaven while aligned with Satan, which is why Jesus emphasized the need to be "Born Again" (John 3:3).

Becoming born again marks our transfer to the Lord's team, where we start to live by His principles. This switch automatically makes us adversaries to Satan, which, understandably, angers him. Imagine how it would feel to lose a star player to your biggest rival, especially if that player starts influencing others to make the same switch.

You would not like it, and neither does the devil. I am convinced that this is the reason why those who really ran with him have so much trouble crossing over and staying on the Lord's team.

Because the enemy knows our value to the Lord, he directs severe attacks against us. Among these, the spirit of offense is one he frequently employs because it can be effective in almost any setting: church, home, work, family, and even among strangers (think road rage). He uses this spirit to both attack and attach itself to us with the ultimate goal of removing us from our rightful position in God.

Satan is a Bully

Since Satan can't defeat the Lord, he acts like a bully, targeting those whom God loves—us. His strategy involves attacking us in hopes that we'll revert to following him again. He aims to influence how we react to offenses, steering us towards responses that align with his destructive playbook rather than the Lord's teachings. The enemy doesn't mind if we identify as being on the Lord's team, as long as he can still manipulate us to act according to his demonic playbook.

So, essentially, one of the ways Satan uses the weapon of offense is as an offensive tool to challenge our obedience to the Lord and His Word. He tempts us to listen to and follow his ways instead of the Lord's.

When the Lord told Adam he was not permitted to eat the fruit from that particular tree, Satan was listening, plotting, and planning, trying to figure out a way to get Adam to disobey what God said and to follow him instead. Slowly and strategically, he began to build his weapon. It is my thought that Satan pulled the trigger of offense on Eve when he told her the only reason the Lord did not want her and Adam to eat from the Tree of Knowledge was because He did not want them to be like Him. Yup, I believe Eve got offended.

I can imagine her saying, "Yeah, that makes sense. Why else wouldn't God want us eating from that tree? He just doesn't want us to be wise like Him. I wonder who He thinks He is? Let me take a bite of that fruit and give some to my husband, too. We'll show Him!" And just like that, the weapon of offense prospered, and we are all still paying the price. Can you see how powerful getting offended can be?

Satan also forms his spiritual weapons as defensive tools to defend against us. Why would he have to do that? Because once a person gives their life to Christ and begins to walk the path the Lord has set for them, they become a threat to the kingdom of darkness. Often, after our lives have been changed, we begin to witness to friends, family members, co-workers, and just about everyone we come in contact with, sometimes without even opening our mouths. With our light shining bright and the benefits that come from being on a winning team, it is not long before others want to leave the enemy's team and join the Lord's.

We should not fool ourselves into thinking that the devil will sit back and allow this to happen without a fight. He won't just let us go and rescue others from his grip. No way! He will start preparing his arsenals and getting ready for battle. This is why we, too, must prepare.

We need to understand the various weapons Satan uses and how we can neutralize them. As previously mentioned, the one without weapons is likely to be defeated by one who is armed. This is a spiritual battle, and we cannot afford to be ignorant of the devil's schemes and tactics. We also cannot expect to win by relying solely on our natural abilities.

When the Lord began teaching me about the spirit of offense, He revealed that it is crafted for many reasons, some of which include making you angry, bitter, and resentful. It's designed to drive you away from all kinds of relationships, whether personal, business, or romantic. It aims to make you withdraw from others, deter you from assisting others, or prevent you from opening up to others so they can assist you.

The weapon of offense is formed to blow your witness by having you respond and act in ways that are contrary to the ways of Christ. It is also formed to make you a loner. Think about it... If you keep getting hurt, you may shut down from people and just choose to be by yourself.

Steal, Kill and Destroy

Long story short, the spirit of offense is formed to steal, kill, and destroy your destiny. You know that you have been allowing the weapon of offense to prosper when you find yourself holding the evidence of broken relationships and dreams, and you are alone. You walked away from people you used to love and who loved you, you no longer attend the church where you were growing and used to enjoy, you quit or got fired from your job because of your interactions with people, you are estranged from your family, and worst of all, from the Lord! All these disconnections happen because you were offended by something that happened.

The spirit of offense plays on our feelings, emotions, and intellect. It is like a self-detonating bomb. Offense in itself does not destroy relationships; it just pulls the pin and waits for you to explode as you follow after and are led by your explosive feelings and emotions.

One of the fruits of the Spirit is self-control, and when you think about the meaning of self-control, it simply means controlling yourself. As believers, we have to get to a place where we are following the leading of the Holy Spirit, not our thinking, our limited understanding, or our emotions.

Seems Right but Is Wrong

"There is a way that appears to be right, but in the end it leads to death." ~Proverbs 14:12. That proverb is powerful when you think about it. It is letting us know there is a way that seems right, but in the end it leads to death. When I think of death, I think of a complete separation from something or someone. It could be physical death, the separation of your spirit from your body, or spiritual death, when our spirits are separated from God (not that He separates from us, but we separate ourselves from Him) as stated in Isaiah 59:2.

Death can be seen in a relationship when you are no longer connected to a person. The death of a vision can come when pursuing your vision causes people to say things that offend you, and you give up your vision. Death can even be seen financially when it seems like we have been separated from our money. Thank God for being the God of Resurrection!

Proverbs 14:12 is letting us know we can think a path is right, but it could lead to death/separation. So I began to think about that. How can you think something is right and yet it be so wrong? The answer? When you are basing your decisions on you and not Him (Jesus). When you are leaning on your own understanding. When you are following your own thoughts, feelings, and emotions instead of following the Word and Spirit of God. You will experience a separation of people, places, and things that were once important to you.

One of my favorite scriptures is Proverbs 3:5-6: "Trust in the LORD with all thine heart; and lean not unto thine own understanding. In all thy ways acknowledge him, and he shall direct thy paths." (KJV). The spirit of offense is hoping that you do not apply Proverbs 3:5-6 to your life because that Proverb is telling us to trust in the LORD with all of our heart. The heart referred to here is the very seat of our emotions. So basically, we are instructed to trust the LORD with everything that is in us and not to lean on our own understanding.

We have to take the time to acknowledge Him so that He can direct our path. Most of the time, as soon as we feel offended by something or someone, we react without thinking. Just that quick, we have followed our own understanding and did not take the time to acknowledge the Lord so that He might direct our steps.

Don't get me wrong, this happens to every one of us at some time or another. However, as you begin to grow spiritually mature, every area should be growing and maturing as well, including how you handle situations.

Feelings or Facts?

Reacting to our feelings without thinking or praying is expected in a person who just got saved and is just now allowing the Word to penetrate their heart. But when you have been walking with the Lord for a couple of years, going to church, reading your Word, and communicating with God regularly through prayer, you should not still be doing and reacting the same way you did before Christ or as a babe in Christ.

We cannot allow the spirit of offense to start talking to our feelings and emotions, and then follow what our emotions are telling us rather than what the Word is telling us to do. When we follow what our emotions are saying, it will lead us to a path that looks right, feels right, and seems right, but in the end, it leads to death.

When I think about how many times I felt this way or that way about something, only to find out I was wrong, I am grateful to have a roadmap (the Word of God). It leads me down the right path to a life more abundant and a lot more stable than what my feelings could ever allow me to achieve.

We have to grasp that the enemy is anti-God, and he is always trying to get us to act, respond, or feel the opposite of how the Lord wants us to respond. He plays on our emotions to get the job done. When we see that, we can understand why we must acknowledge the Lord in all of our ways so that He can direct us.

When Jesus was ministering to His disciples, some of what He was saying was apparently hard to swallow and digest. It went against their intellect, and it just didn't feel right. Jesus asked them, "Does this offend you?" The Bible does not say what their verbal response was, but we can tell from their actions that they were offended because they walked away from Him. Wow! Here Jesus was telling them the truth, and because they got offended, they walked away.

When the truth did not feel comfortable, they walked away from The Way, The Truth, and The Life and instead walked with the wrong way, falsehood, and death. Whenever we choose the path the enemy has laid out for us, this is what we get. The enemy has not changed his tactics; this is what he is still doing because it works! People are still walking away from destiny and divine connections because the enemy was able to bring the spirit of offense in.

We have to wise up and refuse to be moved. We have to realize this weapon has been formed, and we need to do something more than quote a scripture to ensure the weapon truly does not prosper against us.

Recap:

- **The Spirit of Offense is Destructive:** It acts as a self-detonating bomb, using our feelings and emotions to trigger reactions that destroy relationships, opportunities, and even our witness for Christ.

- **The Enemy's Strategy:** Satan forms the weapon of offense to steal, kill, and destroy. He aims to lead us away from God's will by manipulating our emotions and intellect, causing us to react impulsively.

- **The Importance of Discernment:** Just because something feels or seems right doesn't mean it aligns with God's truth. Leaning on our own understanding instead of seeking God's guidance leads to separation and destruction.

- **The Role of Truth:** The truth can feel offensive to those not ready to receive it, but it is necessary for growth and freedom. Keeping a heart ready to accept truth helps us resist offense and stay aligned with God's plan.

- **The Call to Spiritual Maturity:** As we grow in Christ, we must learn to respond to offense with the guidance of the Holy Spirit, rather than reacting based on feelings or limited understanding.

Reflection Questions:

1. Have you experienced moments where offense caused you to react in a way that damaged a relationship or opportunity? What could you have done differently?

_____

_____

_____

2. Are there areas in your life where you tend to lean on your own understanding rather than seeking God's guidance?

_____

_____

_____

3. How do you usually respond when the truth challenges your emotions or perspective?

_____

_____

_____

4. Can you identify situations where the enemy used offense to pull you away from God's will? What steps can you take to guard against this in the future?

_____

_____

_____

5. How can you make sure your heart remains ready to accept the truth, even when it's uncomfortable or difficult to hear?

_____

_____

_____

Action Steps:

- **Pause and Pray:** When you feel offended, take a moment to pray before reacting. Ask the Holy Spirit for discernment and guidance.

- **Guard Your Heart:** Be mindful of how the enemy targets your emotions to lead you astray. Protect your heart by staying rooted in God's Word and truth.

- **Choose Self-Control:** Practice responding thoughtfully rather than reacting impulsively. Remember, self-control is a fruit of the Spirit and a sign of spiritual maturity.

- **Stay Anchored in Truth:** Commit to embracing the truth of God's Word, even when it challenges your feelings or understanding.

- **Seek Accountability:** Surround yourself with spiritually mature believers who can help you process offenses and encourage you to stay focused on God's will.

- **Declare God's Promises:** Meditate on and declare scriptures like Proverbs 3:5-6 and Isaiah 54:17, affirming your trust in God's guidance and protection.

Offense is a weapon the enemy crafts specifically to disrupt your relationship with God, damage your witness, and derail your destiny. Recognizing this weapon and its tactics is the first step in ensuring it doesn't prosper against you. By relying on God's truth, practicing self-control, and staying rooted in the Holy Spirit, you can disarm offense and walk in victory.

Let's commit to choosing God's way over our feelings, guarding our hearts, and trusting Him to guide us through every challenge. Together, let's render the weapon of offense powerless in our lives. Greater is He who is in us than he who is in the world!

Take It or Leave It

Offense is one spirit that you can't just rebuke with Isaiah 54:17—*"No weapon that is formed against thee shall prosper; and every tongue that shall rise against thee in judgment thou shalt condemn. This is the heritage of the servants of the LORD, and their righteousness is of me, saith the LORD"* (KJV)—and expect it to go away. You can declare that scripture all day and night, but at the end of the day, the decision lies with you: will you *take* offense, or will you *leave* it?

What do I mean by that? Imagine I hand you a beautifully wrapped gift box. You have a choice: take it or refuse it. Just because I'm offering it doesn't mean you have to receive or accept it. You can politely decline, saying, "No thanks," and no matter how much I want to give it to you, I can't force you to take it. Similarly, every one of us decides what we are going to accept (take) and what we are going to ignore (refuse).

If you willingly take offense, you can't blame anyone but yourself when you find yourself battling anger, bitterness, or unforgiveness. Yes, someone may have offered you offense, but no one made you take it. By choosing to receive it, you invited all the other emotions that come with it into your heart.

I know what you might be thinking: *"But they shouldn't have said or done that!"* And you're absolutely right. They may have been completely wrong. However, if the spirit of offense was designed to get you out of position, to cause you to act in ways that are not pleasing to the Lord, and you *choose* to take it, then you've allowed it to succeed in its purpose. That makes you just as wrong.

I struggled with this myself because it often felt like people went out of their way to provoke me—saying things or behaving in ways designed to upset or hurt me. And honestly, they probably were. But as long as I allowed their actions to get under my skin, there was no end to the cycle of offense.

I recall a time when I attended a church where the Assistant Pastor seemed to have a personal problem with me. She never directly addressed it, but her looks, comments, and actions told me everything I needed to know—or at least what I *thought* I needed to know. I took offense. And as a result, I began to dislike her, allowing my attitude to shift in ways that no longer reflected Christ.

Before I knew it, I was rolling my eyes at her, avoiding conversations, and justifying my behavior with the thought, *"Well, she doesn't like me, so I don't like her either!"* I allowed my feelings to dictate my actions, and the enemy was having a field day with my attitude.

One day, after church, I prayed and asked the Lord what I should do. I was offended, my behavior wasn't right, and I knew it. The Lord told me to humble myself, attend her women's group, and sow a financial seed into her ministry. At first, I was offended all over again—this time by the Lord! I thought, *"Why should I humble myself when she's the one mistreating me?"* I even imagined God giving me a word of judgment to declare over her. But instead, He was dealing with *me* and my heart.

Reluctantly, I obeyed. I prayed about my attitude, then drove to her home where the women's group was meeting. With a pure heart, I participated in the meeting, sowed into her ministry, and left. After that, I never had another issue with her. I don't know if the Lord dealt with her, but He certainly dealt with me. From that point on, even when I had opportunities to take offense, I refused to pick it up.

When we refuse offense, the enemy realizes he can't use that tactic against us anymore, and he has to move on. On the other hand, when we consistently take offense, we allow him to keep us in a constant state of turmoil. Have you ever met someone who seems to be offended by everything? They're always saying things like, *"Did you just see what they did?"* or *"I know they weren't talking to me!"* These people are stuck on the enemy's merry-go-round because they've never learned how to reject offense.

Think of it this way: if your worst enemy kept handing you bombs disguised as gifts and you kept accepting them, they would keep exploding in your hands. There has to come a point where you recognize the tactic, say "No thanks," and return the package to the sender.

Sadly, I've seen many gifted and anointed individuals allow offense to stagnate their ministries. Taking offense—and failing to make it right—can block your spiritual growth and hinder God's work in your life. The truth is, we are responsible for our actions, including our responses to offense.

If you truly desire to walk in God's power, you must learn to reject offense. And if you do take it, you must humble yourself, repent, and make things right. Speaking from experience, it's far easier to reject offense at the outset than to dig yourself out of the ditch it creates.

The enemy will continue to use people and situations to try to offend you. But when you stop giving him that power, he'll be forced to move on to someone else. The next time offense shows up at your door, recognize it for what it is, and send it back with a sign that says, "Return to sender."

Recap:

- **Offense Is a Choice:** While others may offer offense through their actions or words, it is entirely up to you whether to accept it. Rejecting offense keeps your heart and mind aligned with God's will.

- **Offense Blocks Progress:** Carrying offense hinders spiritual growth, stagnates ministries, and keeps us from walking in God's power.

- **Accountability Matters:** Regardless of someone else's behavior, we are responsible for how we respond. Acting in ways that dishonor God due to offense is our responsibility to correct.

- **The Enemy's Strategy:** Satan uses offense to trap believers in cycles of turmoil, bitterness, and anger. However, when we reject offense, he loses his grip and is forced to abandon that tactic.

- **Prevention Is Better Than Cure:** It is much easier to refuse offense at the outset than to deal with the consequences of accepting it.

Reflection Questions:

1. Are there situations in your life where you've taken offense and allowed it to affect your actions? How can you address them to make things right?

_____

_____

_____

2. How do you typically respond when someone provokes or mistreats you? What steps can you take to react in a way that pleases God?

_____

_____

_____

3. Can you identify patterns where the enemy has used offense to hinder your growth or relationships? How can you break those cycles?

_____

_____

_____

4. What practical strategies can you implement to recognize and reject offense when it arises?

_____

_____

_____

5. How does choosing to leave offense align with your desire to reflect Christ's love and grace to others?

_____

_____

_____

Action Steps:

- **Recognize Offense:** Pay attention to your emotions and thoughts when someone's actions provoke you. Ask yourself if the enemy might be using the situation to plant offense in your heart.

- **Pause and Pray:** Before reacting, pause to pray for discernment and strength. Ask God to help you respond in a way that honors Him.

- **Reject the Gift:** When offense is offered, visualize it as a harmful package you can decline to accept. Say, "No thanks," and leave it with the sender.

- **Humble Yourself:** If you've already taken offense, take responsibility for your actions. Pray, repent, and make amends where necessary to restore peace.

- **Guard Your Heart:** Be intentional about staying rooted in God's Word and allowing the Holy Spirit to guide your responses, especially in challenging situations.

- **Set a New Pattern:** The more you reject offense, the less effective it becomes as a weapon against you. Let the enemy see that his tactics no longer work.

Offense is a weapon designed to derail your spiritual growth and rob you of God's best for your life. But when you refuse to take the bait, you disarm the enemy and maintain your focus on the Lord. Let's commit to being people who reject offense, reflect God's love, and walk in the freedom that comes from leaving burdens behind.

*The next time offense comes knocking, remember your choice: **take it or leave it**. Let's choose to leave it, saints, and watch how God elevates us to greater levels in Him.*

Knowing Your True Enemy

When Jesus said, "Father, forgive them for they know not what they are doing," this statement proves beyond a doubt that He is God. Consider what was going on: He had been betrayed by a close companion, faced death at the hands of those He came to save, endured beatings and mockery, and suffered relentless attempts to discredit His identity. Yet, in the middle of all this torment, He asked God to forgive His tormentors, citing their lack of understanding. Let's be real—only God could be that merciful. Me? I'd probably be calling fire down from Heaven.

When I first heard this story, my immediate thought was, *"Oh, they knew EXACTLY what they were doing!"* How could someone not know they were mercilessly beating an innocent man? They deliberately chose Barabbas, a known murderer, over Jesus, who had only ever helped and healed. They knew their actions were cruel and unjust—so why would Jesus, the all-knowing Son of God, say they didn't know what they were doing?

This question led me to a deeper understanding. Perhaps Jesus was pointing to something we often miss or overlook: the fact that people, even when they hurt us, are not our true enemy.

Understanding the Real Enemy

Jesus endured unimaginable mistreatment, yet He was able to pray for those who persecuted Him because He understood His purpose, His mission, and the reality of spiritual warfare.

He knew His real enemy. While people were the ones physically carrying out the actions, Jesus recognized the greater battle was against Satan, who was working through them. This wasn't merely a human conflict—it was a spiritual battle between good and evil. Jesus knew He was fighting Satan himself and that the people's actions were influenced by demonic forces.

Ephesians 6:12 lays this out clearly: *"For our struggle is not against flesh and blood, but against the rulers, against the authorities, against the powers of this dark world and against the spiritual forces of evil in the heavenly realms."*

Our battle isn't with people—not your coworker who undermines you, your family member who criticizes you, or the friend who betrays you. While people may be the visible source of offense, they are not the root of the problem. The true enemy is Satan and the spiritual forces working behind the scenes.

The Danger of Misidentifying the Enemy

If you don't know who your true enemy is, you'll end up fighting the wrong battle. You'll waste time and energy on people while the enemy continues his work unnoticed.

Yes, the hurt and offense often come through people. It may be your coworker, friend, spouse, or even a spiritual leader. But Scripture is clear: we are not fighting against *flesh and blood*. The enemy uses people as vessels, exploiting their insecurities, pride, unresolved pain, or wounds to accomplish his agenda.

For instance, the devil doesn't possess everyone outright, but he can influence thoughts and emotions, often disguising his whispers as their own thoughts. These individuals may not even realize they are being used.

Personal Reflection

I remember a time when I was deeply hurt by people I trusted—people who were supposed to love and support me. Their actions left me feeling angry, bitter, and questioning their intentions. I thought, *"How could they do this if they cared about me?"*

In my frustration, I prayed and asked God why this was happening. The answer He showed me changed my life: *We are not fighting against people. We are fighting against spiritual forces of evil working behind the scenes.*

The Lord revealed how these forces target people's weaknesses—whether it's pride, insecurity, or past hurts—and use them to bring offense and hurt to others. Even spiritual leaders are not immune.

Unresolved issues in their own lives can leave openings for the enemy to use them as tools of offense.

I realized that while people hurt me, it was the enemy who was behind their actions, working to destroy relationships and pull me out of alignment with God's purpose.

Jesus's Example

Jesus understood this better than anyone. He saw the spiritual influences at work behind the betrayal, abuse, and lies He endured. That's why He could pray for His persecutors and forgive them, even as they nailed Him to a cross.

When we adopt His perspective, it becomes easier to separate the person from the influence driving their actions. This doesn't excuse their behavior, but it allows us to respond in a way that reflects Christ rather than our own hurt.

Why the Enemy Targets Us

The closer someone is to you, the more it hurts when they offend or betray you. The enemy knows this and often targets those relationships to cause the greatest damage.

If a stranger insults you, it's easy to brush off. But if a trusted friend or family member wounds you, it cuts deeply. The enemy uses this tactic to make you feel isolated, bitter, and distrusting of others.

This is why Psalm 118:8 says, *"It is better to trust in the Lord than to put confidence in man."* While relationships are a blessing, we must always recognize that people—no matter how much they love us—are fallible and can be used by the enemy. This is also why we must be selective about whom we allow to be close to us. I am especially cautious around people who are not submitted to the Lord.

Jesus said, *"You will know them by their fruit,"* so I pay close attention to how a person treats others, how they talk about people behind their backs, and whether their life aligns with the Spirit of God. When I see someone displaying behavior contrary to the fruit of the Spirit, I am extra aware. And no, I'm not judging—I'm inspecting their fruit, just like Jesus said we should.

When someone's fruit warns me about them, I take heed. Ignoring those warnings can open the door for unnecessary hurt and offense, which the enemy loves to use to distract and derail us. Staying aware and discerning is not judgment; it's wisdom rooted in God's Word.

Responding Like Christ

When you're tempted to hold on to anger and offense, remember that you, too, have hurt others—intentionally or unintentionally. And most importantly, every one of us has hurt Jesus through our sins. Yet, He forgave us because He understood our nature and the spiritual battle we're caught in.

By following His example, we can learn to reject offense, forgive those who hurt us, and stay focused on God's purpose for our lives.

The Process of Growth

As disciples of Christ, we will face betrayal, lies, and opposition—just as Jesus did. But these experiences are part of our spiritual growth. They teach us to rely on God, discern the true enemy, and respond with grace rather than bitterness.

Transformation requires active participation. If you're not feeding your spirit through prayer, worship, and God's Word, you're passively feeding your flesh. Whichever you feed more will become stronger.

Jesus knew His purpose, His enemy, and how to navigate offenses without being derailed. As we grow in Christ, we must learn to do the same, allowing Him to shape us into His likeness.

Final Thought

When we recognize the true enemy and reject offense, we disarm the devil's schemes and stay aligned with God's will. Remember, people aren't the problem—the spiritual forces influencing them are. Let's follow Jesus's example by forgiving, trusting God, and standing firm in the face of every challenge.

Stay close to the Lord, and He will equip you to handle offense with grace and victory, knowing that the battle belongs to Him.

Recap:

- Jesus's words, *"Father, forgive them, for they know not what they are doing,"* remind us that people are not our true enemy. While their actions may hurt us, they are often unknowingly influenced by spiritual forces working against God's plans.

- Ephesians 6:12 clarifies that our battle is not against flesh and blood but against the rulers, authorities, and powers of darkness operating in the spiritual realm.

- Recognizing the enemy's tactics helps us reject offense and avoid bitterness, keeping our focus on the bigger picture.

- Jesus's example teaches us to pray for those who hurt us, seeing beyond their actions to the spiritual influences behind them.

- The enemy thrives when we harbor offense, but when we refuse to take it, we disarm his strategies and walk in freedom.

Reflection Questions:

1. Can you think of a recent situation where you focused on a person as the problem instead of the spiritual battle behind the scenes? How could seeing them through God's perspective have changed your response?

_____

_____

_____

2. Are there areas in your life where bitterness or offense might have taken root? How can you begin to release those to God?

_____

_____

_____

3. How often do you pray for those who hurt or offend you? What steps can you take to make this a habit?

_____

_____

_____

4. In what ways can you strengthen your spiritual discernment to better recognize the enemy's tactics in your relationships and daily interactions?

_____

_____

_____

5. How does knowing the devil is your true enemy help you approach conflict differently?

_____

_____

_____

Action Steps:

- Commit to responding to offense with prayer instead of anger. Ask God to reveal the bigger picture in every situation.

- Spend time in Ephesians 6:10-18, meditating on the armor of God and how it equips you to fight spiritual battles.

- Make it a daily practice to pray for the people in your life, especially those who challenge you. Ask God to bless them and work in their hearts.

- Evaluate any unresolved hurt or offense in your life, and take intentional steps to forgive and release it to God.

When we remember who the true enemy is, we position ourselves to walk in victory, reflecting Christ's love and grace even in the face of offense.

Mirror, Mirror

A mirror is a surface that reflects the image in front of it. When you stand in front of a mirror, you are not looking to see anyone else except yourself. Besides taking a picture or having someone else tell you what you look like, looking into a mirror is the only way to truly know how you appear.

If a person never takes the time to look in the mirror, they could leave the house looking any ole kind of way without even realizing it. Imagine someone heading to a job interview without first checking their reflection. They might believe they look tidy and professional, but if they had taken the time to look in the mirror, they would have noticed the stain on their shirt, their disheveled hair, and their overall unkempt appearance. Do you think that person would get the job? I doubt it.

The same principle applies to us spiritually. If we don't take the time to examine ourselves spiritually, we could be walking around a disheveled mess without even knowing it. We might think we look like Christ but, in reality, look the complete opposite. That's why we need to hold up a mirror to see who we truly are.

I love when Jesus told His disciples that one of them was going to betray Him, and each of them looked inwardly and asked, "Is it I?" They were willing to examine themselves and see their reflection. They didn't just assume it wasn't them.

As believers in Christ, everything we do and everywhere we go reflects Christ to the world. Our co-workers, neighbors, friends, and family may never read the Bible, but they are reading us daily. Is your chapter helping or hurting people's perception of Christ?

As representatives of the Lord on earth, we must strive to show an authentic representation of Him. This can only happen when we reflect Christ on the inside as well as the outside. Unlike a mirror, which reveals only our outward appearance, an offense will reveal the condition of our hearts.

Offense as a Spiritual Mirror

In the midst of offense, there are lessons about YOU waiting to be learned. Many people don't realize the roots of bitterness, pride, or anger that exist within them until they are exposed.

"The heart is deceitful above all things and beyond cure. Who can understand it?" Jeremiah 17:9.

How we respond to situations reveals our character and spiritual maturity. It speaks louder than anything we or others could say about us. For this reason, the Lord often allows offenses to come our way to expose areas we need to be delivered from or grow in.

Through my experiences, the Lord has used offenses to develop and deepen my relationship with Him. One of the main lessons I had to learn was how to trust Him to defend, protect, and vindicate me. By properly learning how to handle offense, I was able to grow spiritually in ways I never imagined.

The Pride Trap

I used to be someone who always felt the need to defend myself. If someone said something to me, I had to say something back or at least try to explain myself. During this process, I learned that this attitude was rooted in pride. If I truly trusted the Lord, I wouldn't feel the need to constantly prove, validate, or vindicate myself. I needed to trust Him to do that for me.

Pride is what got Satan kicked out of Heaven, and it's often one of the first things the Lord deals with when preparing us for His work. When someone offends us, pride tells us to stand tall and say, "I don't have to take this; I'm out of here!" But what if it's God's will that we stay and endure it? Pride will never consider that possibility.

Jesus didn't have to endure the crucifixion for us, but He did because it was His desire to fulfill the Father's will completely. How many of us are willing to endure whatever is necessary to fulfill the Father's will—not because we have to, but because it's our desire to obey Him?

Offenses Reveal Character

Many of us claim we are humble, but are we really? Offense has a way of sniffing out any pride still lingering in us. God wants us to become totally obedient to His Spirit, not swayed by our feelings and emotions. Offenses challenge us to choose between our will and the Lord's will.

When people hurt, betray, or let us down, do we handle the situation the way we did before we came to Christ, or do we respond as the Lord desires? Offenses test whether we're truly walking in the Fruit of the Spirit or if we're just saying we are.

Instead of getting upset and murmuring, "How could they?" we should be asking the Lord to show us ourselves. This is the perfect time to crucify our flesh even more. Remember, the less there is of us, the more there is of Him operating in our lives.

Self-Reflection Through Offense

Pray and ask the Lord to show you how to respond His way instead of reacting your way. Ask Him to purge any unrighteousness that an offense has exposed or attempted to implant in your heart, mind, and actions. Ask Him to help you prevent the weapon of offense from prospering against you.

This isn't easy. If it were, everyone would do it, and the world would be a better place. But human nature tends to point fingers at others when things go wrong. Remember, when you point a finger at someone else, three fingers point back at you. Each one can represent the Father, the Son, and the Holy Spirit asking: Are you living according to My Word? Are you following My example? Are you allowing Me to lead you?

Every one of us should be asking the Lord to examine and purify our hearts. Don't be surprised if numerous offenses come your way as a result. Often, we don't realize we have an issue until something happens to expose it.

Learning Through Offenses

Consider Peter. He genuinely believed he would never deny Christ, but when the moment of testing came, he did exactly what Jesus said he would. Peter's denial shocked and horrified him, but it taught him a valuable lesson. Once Peter recognized his mistake, he repented, learned, and never made that same mistake again.

Similarly, when the Lord reveals a character flaw through offense, it's not to condemn us but to help us grow. Offenses provide opportunities for us to learn and become more like Christ.

The Power of Self-Denial

Jesus said in Matthew 16:24, "Whoever wants to be my disciple must deny themselves and take up their cross daily and follow me." This life of self-denial means we must lay down our right to react even when we feel justified in doing so. Instead, we respond with the humility and grace of Christ.

When you look in the mirror, who do you see? Do you see the person you used to be, defending your emotional rights? Or do you see someone transformed by Christ, trusting Him to handle the battle?

Everyone knows who you used to be and what you're capable of when left to yourself. But who are you now? Let your life reflect the transformation Christ has made in you.

Mirror, mirror on the wall, who is the most humble of them all?

Recap:

- **Offenses as Spiritual Mirrors:** Offenses reveal the condition of our hearts, exposing areas of pride, bitterness, or anger we may not recognize otherwise.

- **Revealing Character:** How we respond to offenses highlights our spiritual maturity. Following Christ requires us to choose His way over our emotions.

- **Pride's Role:** Pride often drives our reactions to offense, but true growth comes from humbling ourselves and trusting God to defend and vindicate us.

- **Learning Through Exposure:** The Lord uses offenses to uncover flaws, not to condemn us, but to refine and transform us.

- **The Power of Self-Denial:** A true disciple of Christ lays down their right to react negatively and instead responds with humility and grace.

- **Reflecting Christ:** Our actions and attitudes serve as a reflection of Christ to the world. When we handle offenses well, we testify of His transforming power.

Reflection Questions:

1. When offense arises, do you react out of pride, or do you seek to respond with humility and grace?

_____

_____

_____

2. What lessons has God taught you through recent offenses?

_____

_____

_____

3. Are you allowing the Lord to examine your heart and reveal areas needing growth, or are you resisting the process?

_____

_____

_____

4. In what ways can you trust God more fully to handle situations that provoke offense?

_____

_____

_____

5. How can your response to offense better reflect Christ to those around you?

_____

_____

_____

Action Steps:

- **Pause and Reflect:** Before reacting to an offense, take a moment to pray and ask the Lord for guidance. Invite Him to reveal what the situation is exposing in your heart.

- **Choose Self-Denial:** Make a conscious decision to deny your right to react negatively. Instead, respond in a way that reflects Christ's humility and love.

- **Seek Growth Through Offense:** When offenses reveal character flaws, bring them to the Lord in prayer. Ask Him to cleanse your heart and help you grow in those areas.

- **Practice Trust:** Trust the Lord to vindicate and defend you. Let go of the need to prove yourself, relying instead on His justice and timing.

- **Commit to Reflection:** Regularly examine your heart and actions, ensuring they align with God's Word and the Fruit of the Spirit.

Offenses are opportunities for growth, reflection, and transformation. When we view them as spiritual mirrors, we can see ourselves more clearly and align our lives more closely with Christ. Let's commit to becoming more like Him, trusting that every offense we face can lead to deeper maturity and greater reflection of His love.

The next time you look in the mirror—spiritually or physically—ask yourself: **Am I reflecting Christ to the world?** *Then, let your life answer with a resounding* **yes.**

Helping Others Get It Right

Offenses also reveal truths to others, helping them recognize their own flaws so they, too, can get it right. Ministry is not fun and games; it is about denying your will so the Lord's will can be accomplished. It is about laying down your life for your brothers and sisters in Christ. Jesus said, "Greater love has no one than this, than to lay down one's life for his friends."

I believe this scripture applies literally as well as spiritually. How many of us would be willing to endure offense so that another person could be made whole? Even people who love us can sometimes be used to hurt us.

How many would be willing to overlook a loved one's actions when they do something hurtful? I often think about the story of David and Saul. Saul had issues, especially with jealousy, which led him to try to kill David multiple times. Yet, despite Saul's behavior, David loved him regardless. Let me say that again: Despite Saul's actions, David loved him regardless.

When the tables turned, and David had the opportunity to take revenge, he didn't. When Saul realized that David had spared his life, he broke down crying and acknowledged David's righteousness, saying David was more righteous than he was (1 Samuel 24). Through David's response, Saul was forced to see himself, at least for a moment.

I want to remind you: the people who hurt you—God will deal with them. When you respond in the right way, the Lord will elevate you and crown you before their eyes. He has a way of letting everyone, including you, know how proud He is of your obedience!

When this happens, it forces people to reflect on their actions and words. If they are serious about their relationship with the Lord, they will feel compelled to get it right with Him and with you.

Not many people want to be a whipping board, but Jesus was. The more you desire to be like Him, the more you will find yourself enduring similar situations. The key is responding the way He did.

Let me add a disclaimer: this principle should not be taken out of context. It is important to remain prayerful and watchful at all times. I do not believe the Lord will keep you in a situation where you are continuously abused in any way just for someone else's deliverance. Even David fled when Saul actively tried to harm him, but he forgave Saul when Saul repented.

Sometimes, we shouldn't be so quick to get offended and abandon someone just because they did or said something we didn't like. You have to discern through prayer when it's time to leave and when it's time to stay. When we get offended, our first instinct is often to leave or retaliate, but we need to seek the Lord's guidance.

There have been times when someone's tone or words hurt me, but before pride could take over, the Holy Spirit would whisper, "Don't get upset, just listen." In those moments, I would find that the person was hurting or going through a difficult time. By overlooking the offense, I was able to help them experience breakthrough—and sometimes, I received a blessing in return.

I cannot count how many times I've had to overlook offenses. Although it was painful at times, I was always glad I did when I saw the blessings of restored friendships and divine connections that came as a result. Many people are hurting and feel unlovable. Overlooking offenses can help heal them and show them they are loved.

This aspect of ministry is something many people haven't tapped into. It's easy to love those who love us or to minister to those who receive us, but what about the ones God sends who are so broken they can't even love themselves? Can you see beyond the coal to discover the diamond? Are you willing to invest your time so someone else can feel the love of Christ through you? That is true ministry and the only real way to demonstrate Christ's unconditional love.

How Anointed Are You?

One of my sayings is this: If you're really anointed, you should be able to love the hell out of your enemies—literally. I say this not as a curse but as the truth. Can you love someone so deeply that the darkness, torment, or hell within them is replaced by Christ's light? Jesus did it for us, and with His power working in you, you can do it too.

Think about this: How do you feel when people leave you just because you said or did something that inadvertently offended them? Maybe you were having a bad day, a bad week, or even a bad year. Have you ever been overwhelmed spiritually, emotionally, or personally, and lashed out at someone undeserving of your frustration? Afterward, you might feel guilty, but what if that relationship was damaged because they walked away offended? This is why it's crucial to be Holy Spirit-led, not emotionally driven.

We all make mistakes and hurt others, sometimes unknowingly. The same mercy we want others to extend to us, we must be willing to extend to them.

There have been times in my walk with the Lord when I stayed connected to people I would have preferred to walk away from. People I knew were dishonest or unkind. Yet, the Lord kept me connected to them. At first, I couldn't understand why, but eventually, I began to see the bigger picture.

It's easy to love those who treat us well, but it takes the Holy Spirit to love those who don't. Luke 6:32-35 says:

"If you love those who love you, what credit is that to you? Even sinners love those who love them. And if you do good to those who are good to you, what credit is that to you? Even sinners do that. And if you lend to those from whom you expect repayment, what credit is that to you? Even sinners lend to sinners, expecting to be repaid in full. But love your enemies, do good to them, and lend to them without expecting to get anything back. Then your reward will be great, and you will be children of the Most High, because He is kind to the ungrateful and wicked."

What Grade Are You Getting on Your Test?

The true test of Christ-like love is loving our enemies. This scripture also reminds us that our reward for doing so will be great! I know loving our enemies and those who offend us is hard. It's impossible in our own strength, but with Christ, all things are possible. A non-Christian loves through their own ability, but Christians love through the ability God gives them. Love is a fruit of the Spirit, just like joy, peace, patience, kindness, goodness, gentleness, faithfulness, and self-control. These fruits manifest when circumstances would naturally produce the opposite.

Think about this:

1. **Enduring Offenses to Help Others:**
   o Enduring offenses with grace can lead others to self-reflection and growth.
   o Our response to offenses serves as a testimony of God's love in us.

2. **Loving the Hell Out of People:**

   o   Loving deeply can dispel the darkness in others and reveal Christ's transformative power.

3. **Loving Beyond Reciprocity:**

   o   True Christ-like love is unconditional, extending even to those who oppose us.

4. **The Spirit of God Empowers Us:**

   o   The Holy Spirit enables us to love and forgive beyond our natural capacity.

5. **Ministering Unconditional Love:**

   o   God may call us to minister to those who are difficult to love. Obeying Him in this reflects true discipleship.

6. **Extending Mercy and Forgiveness:**

   o   Remember how often we've needed mercy. Extend that same grace to others.

7. **Trusting God's Timing:**

   o   Trust that God sees your circumstances and will intervene at the right time.

Recap:

- **Enduring Offenses as Ministry:** Offenses can serve a greater purpose, helping others see their flaws and inspiring them to seek change.

- **True Ministry:** True ministry involves loving others, even in their brokenness, and showing them the unconditional love of Christ.

- **Reflecting Christ's Love:** The ability to love and forgive, even those who offend us, is a hallmark of Christ-like character.

- **Mercy and Grace:** The mercy we seek from others is the same mercy we must extend to them.

- **Trusting God's Sovereignty:** God will deal with those who hurt us. Our role is to trust His timing and His methods, whether it's to remove them or redeem the relationship.

Reflection Questions:

1. Have you experienced a time when enduring an offense led to a positive change in someone else's life?

_____

_____

_____

2. Are there difficult relationships where God is calling you to stay and show His love, even when it's hard?

_____

_____

_____

3. How do you respond when people hurt or offend you? Does your response reflect Christ's love?

_____

_____

_____

4. In what ways can you extend mercy to someone who has wronged you?

_____

_____

_____

5. How can you trust God more fully to handle difficult situations and relationships?

_____

_____

_____

Action Steps:

- **Seek the Lord's Guidance:** Before reacting to an offense, pray and ask God for wisdom. Let Him guide your response.

- **Show Mercy:** Think of someone who has hurt you. Take a step toward reconciliation by extending forgiveness or kindness.

- **Reflect Christ's Love:** Make it a point to love others, especially those who challenge you. Ask the Holy Spirit to help you see them through God's eyes.

- **Trust God's Timing:** Resist the urge to take matters into your own hands. Trust that God will act at the right time.

- **Practice Patience:** Commit to enduring difficult situations with grace, knowing that your response can inspire others to seek God.

Helping others get it right often requires us to endure, forgive, and love in ways that challenge our natural inclinations. By allowing God to work through us, we can become instruments of healing and transformation. The next time you're faced with an offense, ask yourself: **How can I use this moment to reflect Christ's love and draw others closer to Him?**

Let your life be a living testimony of God's grace, showing that His love is powerful enough to overcome even the deepest offenses.

Father, Who Are You?

"It was good for me to be afflicted so that I might learn your decrees." Psalm 119:71. Offenses reveal another dimension of who God is and the power that lies within His Word. How would you know the Lord is a healer if you were never sick? How would you know the Lord as a provider if you never had a need? How can the Word come alive to you if you never had to test it and hold on to it when you were going through hell?

No one wants to go through a bad experience, yet we all want the benefits that come from them. The Lord loves to reveal Himself, and offenses are a prime opportunity for Him to show Himself as a Heart Healer, Mind Regulator, Prince of Peace, Vindicator, Reconciler, and so much more. When you endure offenses, you will see the Lord as your protector and witness how He moves and deals with people who hurt you.

I remember someone disliking me for reasons I didn't know at the time (I later found out it was because the pastor, of all people, was speaking negatively about me to them). One day at church, this person said and did some very hurtful things to me. I was so upset that all I could do was cry in my car and tell the Lord how much I was hurting. Not even twenty-four hours later, I received a call and an apology from that person. Something bad had happened to them, and they believed it was because of how they had mistreated me. From that day forward, they never treated me badly again.

That was just one of many times the Lord dealt with people concerning how they treated me when I LET HIM HANDLE IT instead of trying to handle it myself. Those experiences taught me to trust that the Lord is my vindicator and protector, just as His Word says He is. Was it hard? Absolutely. Was it worth it? Oh, God, yes!

Let Him Handle It

When we get offended or upset by someone's actions, our flesh wants to respond. We want to cuss people out, fight, ignore them, or avoid them entirely. I'm not going to lie—before I submitted to the Lord, I would argue, fuss, and fight. It wasn't easy for me to learn to keep my mouth shut and let the Lord fight my battles.

To help myself, I wrote out scriptures like, "The battle is not yours, it is the Lord's" (2 Chronicles 20:15) and "Vengeance is mine; I will repay, saith the Lord" (Romans 12:19). I memorized them and prayed them whenever I felt the urge to respond in anger. This practice not only helped me internalize scripture but also transformed my mindset from worldly to godly. The Lord was preparing me for the blessings He had in store, but I had to be processed and renewed first. Knowing how to handle offenses is just one stage of preparation for His promises.

Transformation Takes Time

Salvation doesn't mean instant transformation. Spiritual growth happens through reading, meditating on, and applying the Word of God to our lives. Opportunities to apply the Word often come through offenses. These moments test whether we've truly absorbed what we've heard in church or read in the Bible.

When I felt like telling people off, I redirected my focus to the Lord. Instead of venting my frustrations about others, I began telling God how much I loved and trusted Him. This shift deepened my relationship with Him and reinforced my dependence on His strength and wisdom. I often found myself saying, "Father, if You don't handle this, nothing will change."

A Righteous Judge

The Lord is a righteous judge. He deals with everyone, no matter their title, position, or power. Some people think they can get away with anything because of their authority or status, but God's justice sees through all of that. Those in leadership positions have an even greater responsibility to walk in righteousness, as they will be judged more harshly (James 3:1).

It's important to understand that God's purpose isn't about making people suffer for their wrongs but about teaching them lessons. If someone learns their lesson, we should be content with that rather than seeking their downfall. Holding onto images of their punishment only breeds bitterness.

Let's be real—when someone hurts us, our natural inclination is to want revenge. We want them to suffer as we have. But if we don't cast down those thoughts, bitterness will take root. We must trust that God sees everything and has a plan for everyone involved.

Move On

People may never apologize for what they did, but so what? Move on. Just as we can't move forward into God's blessings without obedience, neither can they. The Bible says, "You reap what you sow" (Galatians 6:7). Rest assured, they will reap what they've sown, whether good or bad.

I've experienced deep hurts and betrayals, especially from church leaders, but those moments taught me about the depths of God's love and faithfulness. He always came to my defense and dealt with those who wronged me. Interestingly, He didn't reveal how He handled them until I had forgiven them and moved on. When I did find out, all I could say was, "Wow, Lord, You didn't let them get away with it."

Calling Through Offenses

The Lord also uses offenses to reveal our callings. I remember confiding in leaders about personal struggles, only to find out later they had gossiped about me. It hurt deeply, but the Lord used those experiences to teach me three key lessons:

1. He would deliver me from my struggles, and others would see His transformative power in my life.

2. He called me to a life of transparency, which would bring healing and deliverance to others.

3. As a future leader, I was to protect the privacy and dignity of those who confided in me.

Had I not gone through those betrayals, I wouldn't have known how strong God was in me. I saw how He elevated me above my enemies and opened doors they couldn't enter.

Be Encouraged

If the enemy is targeting you through people you respect, it's because you're a threat to his kingdom. Don't let him win. Lift your head high, forgive, and move forward. Let them talk—your testimony will inspire and deliver others.

The Bible assures us that offenses will come but warns woe to those who bring them (Matthew 18:7). Rest in the knowledge that your Heavenly Father fights for you. In His presence, you will find peace, comfort, and encouragement.

As you grow in intimacy with the Lord, you'll see yourself maturing spiritually. You'll realize that what once hurt you no longer fazes you.

Think About This:

1. **Offenses Reveal God's Dimensions:**
   o Challenges allow us to experience God's attributes, such as healing, provision, and protection.
   o Witnessing God's power in action strengthens our faith and reliance on Him.

2. **Letting God Fight Your Battles:**
   o Trusting God with conflicts demonstrates faith in His sovereignty.

- Stepping back lets us see God's hand at work in ways we couldn't orchestrate ourselves.

3. **Redirecting Emotions to God:**
   - Venting frustrations to God transforms our perspective and draws us closer to Him.
   - Focusing on God's greatness shifts our attention from hurt to healing.

4. **Trusting and Letting Go:**
   - Surrendering control brings peace and assurance that God is in charge.
   - Dependence on God helps us release bitterness and embrace His plans.

5. **Purpose in Suffering:**
   - God uses suffering to teach and mold both us and those who wrong us.
   - Trusting His justice allows us to let go of vengeance and focus on growth.

6. **God's Impartial Judgment:**
   - Titles and positions hold no weight in God's judgment. His justice is righteous and fair.
   - Trusting God's timing ensures we don't carry the burden of seeking retribution.

Recap:

- **Offenses Reveal God's Character:** Through challenges and hurtful experiences, we gain a deeper understanding of who God is—our Healer, Provider, Protector, Vindicator, and more.

- **Trusting God to Fight Battles:** When we let go of the urge to retaliate and allow God to handle situations, we witness His justice and faithfulness.

- **Redirecting Emotions:** Turning frustrations into declarations of love and trust in God strengthens our relationship with Him and aligns us with His peace.

- **Releasing Bitterness:** Trusting God's justice allows us to let go of the weight of vengeance and embrace forgiveness.

- **God's Purpose in Offenses:** Every offense has a purpose, often to teach us, reveal our calling, and prepare us for greater blessings.

- **God's Justice is Impartial:** Titles, positions, or power cannot shield anyone from God's righteous judgment.

Reflection Questions:

1. How have recent offenses revealed a new dimension of who God is in your life?

   _____

   _____

   _____

2. Are there situations where you need to let God fight your battles instead of reacting?

   _____

   _____

   _____

3. How can you redirect your emotions toward God when dealing with hurt or betrayal?

   _____

   _____

   _____

4. What lessons has God taught you through offenses? How have these lessons prepared you for His greater purpose?

_____

_____

_____

5. Are you holding onto bitterness that needs to be released? How can you trust God's justice in that situation?

_____

_____

_____

Action Steps:

- **Memorize Key Scriptures:** Write down and memorize verses like 2 Chronicles 20:15 ("The battle is not yours, but God's") and Romans 12:19 ("Vengeance is mine; I will repay, says the Lord"). Use them as reminders to trust God in difficult moments.

- **Pray for Those Who Hurt You:** Lift up the people who have wronged you in prayer. Ask God to work in their hearts and use the situation for His glory.

- **Focus on God's Attributes:** When facing challenges, meditate on the attributes of God you've experienced— Healer, Provider, Protector—and thank Him for His faithfulness.

- **Journal Your Journey:** Reflect on how God has handled situations where you let Him fight your battles. Use these moments as testimonies of His goodness.

- **Release Bitterness:** Consciously choose to let go of bitterness by confessing it to God and asking Him to replace it with His peace.

- **Seek God's Purpose:** Ask the Lord to reveal how He is using current or past offenses to teach and prepare you for His calling.

Offenses are inevitable, but they are also opportunities to grow in faith and maturity. Each challenge reveals more about God's nature and strengthens our trust in His plans. By letting go of control, trusting His justice, and focusing on His greatness, we transform pain into purpose and reflect His glory in our lives.

Let every offense draw you closer to the Father, knowing that He is working all things together for your good and His glory.

Things Aren't Always What They Seem

*F*rom the very beginning, Satan has always been a liar and deceiver. He specializes in making things appear a certain way, and the moment we react or respond based on his deception, we realize we've been fooled. He uses this strategy in many areas of our lives, including through offenses.

What am I talking about? How many times have you believed someone had a problem with you, only to find out later you couldn't have been more wrong? So many relationships are ruined before they even have a chance to begin simply because the enemy loves to twist people's words, actions, and mannerisms into something they're not.

I remember ministering at the local county jail with another woman. A young girl joined us a few minutes after we had started. For some reason, she stared at me as if she had a problem with me, giving me the dirtiest looks ever! I had to fight the urge to return her glare. Instead, I told myself, "Ayanna, you are here to minister the Word of God; you cannot get upset because someone is staring you up and down."

After we finished ministering, the woman I was with said, "The Lord told me to have you pray for that girl and lead her to the Lord." Of course, she was talking about the girl giving me those dirty looks. I silently prayed for strength and approached her. When I asked if I could pray with her, she said yes and accepted the Lord as her Savior. Minutes later, a familiar feeling came over me, and I asked her, "Do I know you?" She responded, "I was going to ask you the same thing." Suddenly, she exclaimed, "You were my nurse when I got shot four years ago, and you told me about Jesus then."

Instantly, I remembered taking care of a 17-year-old girl who had been shot in her buttocks and witnessing to her about Jesus. That 17-year-old girl was her! We hugged and burst into tears.

Now, imagine if I had gotten offended and responded to what I thought were nasty looks. The enemy was playing on my feelings, making me interpret her stares as confrontational when she was just trying to figure out why I seemed familiar. I am so grateful I didn't let myself go down the path the enemy was leading me.

The Danger of Misinterpretation

If anyone knows me, they know I use social media frequently to post inspirational and motivational messages. Occasionally, I post messages of correction, but they are never directed at anyone in particular. Yet, I cannot tell you how many people have believed I was talking about them!

Once, someone I didn't know sent me a message claiming I was talking about someone we both knew. I had to laugh. She had never interacted with me, yet she thought she knew the intent behind my post. That was either her imagination or the enemy making things seem like something they weren't.

I've also had someone I considered a little brother assume a sermon I preached was about him. He claimed I kept looking at him while I preached, and that convinced him the message was directed at him. I couldn't even remember what the message was about, but whatever it was must have applied to his life. Unfortunately, instead of receiving it, he chose to find fault and get offended. Our relationship was never the same.

Overcoming Negative Thoughts

When the enemy tries to convince me someone is being rude or trying to throw shade, I choose to cast those thoughts down. I say to myself, "I'm not going there." We face enough real warfare daily without adding unnecessary conflict.

I'd rather think everyone loves me and be wrong than think everyone hates me and be wrong. At least in my fantasy world, I'm happy! People who are constantly suspicious think everyone is out to get them. They live miserable lives, with poor relationships and walls around their hearts. Even if they claim to be content, they're not. No matter how many bad experiences I've had, I refuse to let them stop my love flow.

Who knows? It could be the enemy's plan to send all the wrong people your way—pastors, friends, spouses, or business associates—to keep you from opening your heart to the right ones.

Guarding Your Mind

The Word of God instructs us on how to replace negative thoughts with positive ones:

"Finally, brothers and sisters, whatever is true, whatever is noble, whatever is right, whatever is pure, whatever is lovely, whatever is admirable—if anything is excellent or praiseworthy—think about such things." Philippians 4:8.

By focusing on these positive attributes, we can guard our hearts and minds against the enemy's deceptions. We maintain a heart of love, openness, and positivity, allowing God's light to shine through us.

Think About This:

1. **Admitting Perceptual Errors:**
    o   Be humble enough to recognize your perception might be flawed. This openness prevents unnecessary misunderstandings.
    o   Clear communication strengthens relationships and builds trust.

2. **Casting Down Negative Thinking:**
    o   Replace negative thoughts with positive, faith-filled ones. This practice guards your heart and aligns your thinking with God's truth.
    o   Mental discipline helps you stay focused on God's perspective rather than the enemy's lies.

3. **The Enemy's Deception:**

   o Satan thrives on making things appear worse or different than they are. Stay vigilant and discerning.

   o Pray for wisdom to see through deception and maintain a truthful perspective.

4. **Reflecting on Misinterpretations:**

   o Remember times when others misunderstood your intentions. Use those experiences to foster empathy and patience.

   o Give others the benefit of the doubt, just as you would want for yourself.

5. **Avoiding Assumptions:**

   o Don't jump to conclusions about someone's intentions. Instead, focus on clear communication and seek clarification when needed.

   o Avoiding assumptions reduces conflict and promotes peace.

6. **Choosing Positive Thoughts:**

   o Positive thinking creates a healthy, loving environment. Trust that God will reveal the truth if needed.

   o Let your thoughts reflect Philippians 4:8, focusing on what is true, noble, right, pure, lovely, admirable, excellent, and praiseworthy.

Recap:

- **Admit Perceptions Can Be Wrong:** It's easy to misinterpret actions or words, but admitting you could be mistaken prevents unnecessary conflict.

- **Cast Down Negative Thoughts:** Even valid-seeming negative thoughts can be deceptions planted by the enemy. Reject them and align your thinking with God's truth.

- **The Enemy's Deception:** Satan thrives on twisting reality, making things appear worse or different than they are.

- **Reflect on Misinterpretations:** Remember times when others misunderstood you and extend the same grace to others.

- **Avoid Assumptions:** Unless someone directly addresses you, don't assume their actions or words are about you.

- **Think Positively:** It's better to think the best about others and be wrong than to assume the worst and be wrong. Trust God to reveal the truth and guide your response.

Reflection Questions:

1. Can you recall a time when your perception of someone's actions or words was proven wrong? How did it affect the situation?

_____

_____

_____

2. What steps can you take to replace negative thoughts with positive, faith-filled ones?

_____

_____

_____

3. How often do you reflect on how others may have misinterpreted your actions? How can this reflection help you be more empathetic?

_____

_____

_____

4. Do you find yourself making assumptions about people's intentions? What can you do to seek clarity instead?

_____

_____

_____

5. How can focusing on Philippians 4:8 help you guard your thoughts and maintain a heart of love?

_____

_____

_____

Action Steps:

- **Pause Before Reacting:** When negative thoughts arise, take a moment to pray and ask God to reveal the truth of the situation.

- **Memorize Philippians 4:8:** Write it down and recite it daily to guide your thinking and align your thoughts with God's Word.

- **Practice Empathy:** Reflect on times when your actions were misinterpreted and use those experiences to extend grace to others.

- **Communicate Clearly:** If you sense tension or confusion in a relationship, seek clarification in a loving and non-confrontational way.

- **Cultivate Positivity:** Make a conscious decision to assume the best about others, trusting God to handle any misjudgments.

The enemy thrives on deception, but by choosing to admit our flaws, cast down negative thoughts, and seek God's perspective, we can overcome his schemes. Let your interactions reflect Christ's love and truth, fostering peace and understanding in every relationship.

"Father, help me see people and situations through Your eyes. Guard my heart against deception and guide my thoughts to align with Your Word."

Love That Transforms

*L*et me tell you something powerful about enduring offenses with grace—it's not just about you getting stronger. Every time you handle offense God's way, you're holding up a mirror for someone else to see themselves. I've seen it happen time and time again—when you respond to hurt with love instead of retaliation, it makes people stop and think, "Why aren't they responding the way I would?"

Think about it: When someone expects you to blow up, walk away, or strike back, but instead you show love and patience, it confuses them. That confusion? That's the Holy Spirit using your response to work on their heart. Your restraint becomes their revelation.

I remember a situation where a coworker was constantly trying to undermine me. Every meeting, every email, every chance they got—they were there trying to make me look bad. My flesh wanted to expose them, defend myself, and give them a piece of my mind. But the Holy Spirit kept telling me, "Show them My love instead."

It wasn't easy—let me tell you that right now! But as I kept choosing to respond with kindness and excellence, something started happening. Not only did others begin to see the truth, but that coworker started changing. One day, they came to me in tears, apologizing. They said, "I couldn't understand why you were still kind to me when I was being so awful. It made me look at myself, and I didn't like what I saw."

Loving the Hell Out

Now, when I say "loving the hell out of people," I'm not being crude—I'm being real. There's a darkness in people that can only be driven out by light. And guess what? We're called to be that light! When Jesus said to let your light shine, He wasn't talking about just being nice. He was talking about a love so powerful it drives out darkness.

Think about Jesus and the demoniac. Everyone else had given up on him, chained him up, and left him among the tombs. But Jesus saw past the demons to the person God created. That's what I mean by looking beyond the coal to see the diamond.

Let me show you what this looks like in real life. Maybe there's someone in your church who's always gossiping or causing division. Instead of avoiding them or gossiping back, what if you started praying for them? What if you asked God to show you what He sees when He looks at them? What if you began to speak life over them instead of speaking about them?

Beyond Feel-Good Love

Here's where it gets real. Anyone can love someone who's loving them back. That's not special—that's just human nature. But loving someone who's actively trying to hurt you? That's supernatural. That's God-level love.

When Jesus said to love your enemies, He wasn't suggesting something nice to try when we feel like it. He was giving us a command that would set us apart from the world. The world says, "Love those who love you." Jesus says, "Love those who hate you."

Let me give you some real-world examples of what this supernatural love looks like:

When Love Doesn't Feel Natural

I had a situation in ministry where someone was spreading lies about me. Not just little misunderstandings—I'm talking about malicious, calculated stories meant to destroy my reputation. My natural response? I wanted to gather all my evidence, expose their lies, and defend myself. That would have been the "normal" thing to do, right?

But the Holy Spirit challenged me: "Will you love them through this? Will you show them what My love looks like?"

So instead of defending myself, I:

- Continued to speak well of them even when others brought up the rumors

- Prayed for their success and blessing (and let me tell you, that was HARD at first!)

- Looked for opportunities to serve them

- Refused to join in when others criticized them

Was it easy? Not at all. Did it feel good? Nope. But here's what happened—over time, that person began to change. Not because I convinced them they were wrong, but because God's love broke through their defenses.

The Power of Spirit-Enabled Love

Here's the thing about loving like this—you can't do it in your own strength. I've tried, and I've failed. This kind of love only comes through the power of the Holy Spirit working in you.

When someone has hurt you deeply, you can't just decide to love them. You have to:

1. Acknowledge your hurt to God

2. Ask Him to help you see that person through His eyes

3. Rely on His strength, not your own

4. Choose to act in love even when your feelings haven't caught up

5. Keep doing it, even when you don't see immediate results

I remember praying, "Lord, I can't love this person. I don't even want to love this person. But You can love them through me." That's when things started to change—not just in them, but in me.

The Ministry of Difficult Love

Sometimes God will specifically place you in situations or relationships with difficult people. Why? Because He knows that your ability to love them might be their only glimpse of His love.

Think about it this way: If you're in a room full of darkness and you light just one candle, where does everyone look? At the light! When you show supernatural love in a situation that calls for natural hatred, people notice. They might not say anything at first, but they notice.

I've seen this play out in:

- Family relationships where there's been deep hurt
- Church situations where there's been betrayal
- Workplace environments filled with rivalry
- Community settings where there's division

In each case, choosing to love when others choose hate becomes a powerful testimony. It's not about being a doormat—it's about being a demonstration of God's love in action.

You see, when you love someone who's hurt you, you're not just affecting that one relationship. You're showing everyone watching that there's a different way to handle offense. You're demonstrating that God's love is more powerful than human hurt.

This kind of love:

- Breaks down walls others have built
- Heals wounds that logic can't touch
- Changes situations that seem hopeless
- Transforms both the giver and receiver

Remember, Jesus didn't just tell us to love our enemies—He showed us how by loving us when we were His enemies. Every time you choose to love someone who's hurt you, you're participating in that same divine pattern.

Love in Action: Making It Real

Let me get practical with you about how to show this kind of transformative love in everyday situations. This isn't just theory—this is where the rubber meets the road.

In Church Settings

You know those moments after service when you see someone coming who's been talking about you? Instead of ducking into the bathroom or suddenly becoming very interested in your phone:

- Make eye contact and smile genuinely
- Walk over and greet them warmly
- Ask about their family or something personal they've mentioned before
- Offer to pray with them if they share a concern

I remember one Sunday when a sister who had been criticizing my teaching style approached me. Instead of being cold or distant, I asked her to coffee. During our conversation, I discovered she was dealing with deep hurt from her past ministry experiences. That coffee meeting turned into a healing moment for both of us.

At Work

When that coworker takes credit for your work or throws you under the bus in meetings:

- Keep doing excellent work without drawing attention to yourself
- Support their good ideas in meetings
- Share helpful information they might need
- Offer to help when they're struggling with a project

I had a supervisor who constantly belittled my ideas in meetings. Instead of getting bitter, I started sending her encouraging notes about her leadership strengths. Two months later, she broke down in my office and shared she was dealing with intense pressure from upper management. My kindness had been breaking down walls she'd built from fear.

In Family Situations

Family hurt can be the deepest because they know exactly where to stick the knife. When dealing with difficult family members:

- Show up at family events with a genuine heart to bless
- Remember important dates and acknowledge them
- Share good memories that remind them of better times
- Be the first to reach out after disagreements

One of the hardest tests of love came when a family member spread private information about me to others. The Holy Spirit told me to send them a birthday gift anyway—something thoughtful that showed I still cared about their interests. That gift became a bridge to restoration.

With Church Leadership

When leaders make decisions you don't agree with or seem to overlook you:

- Continue serving faithfully
- Pray for them specifically by name
- Support new initiatives even if they weren't your idea
- Find ways to make their job easier

The Daily Choice

This kind of love isn't a one-time decision—it's a daily choice. Every morning, I pray:

- "Lord, help me see people through Your eyes today."
- "Show me opportunities to love difficult people."
- "Give me strength to respond in love when I'm hurt."
- "Let Your love flow through me, especially when I don't feel loving."

Remember, love isn't what you feel—it's what you do. Jesus didn't feel like going to the cross, but He chose love anyway. You might not feel like showing love to that difficult person, but you can choose to act in love regardless of your feelings.

Every time you choose love over offense:

- You're growing more like Christ

- You're breaking down walls in others

- You're creating space for God to work

- You're building your spiritual strength

- You're showing others what God's love looks like

Don't get discouraged if you don't see changes right away. Sometimes the seeds of love we plant take time to grow. Just keep planting. Keep loving. Keep choosing God's way over your feelings. The harvest will come.

Communication: The Bridge that Heals

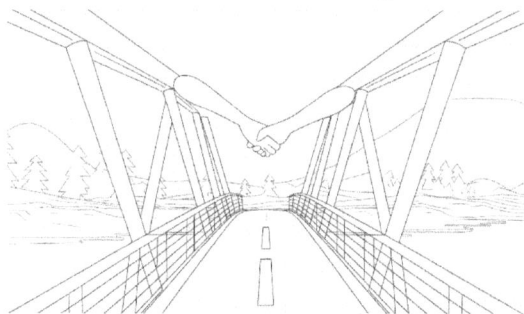

The Weapon of Communication

One of the most powerful weapons that can be used to destroy the spirit of offense is communication. The enemy loves for us to focus on the emotional damage of offense, but the Lord wants us to know that He is a healer and restorer.

As I mentioned in previous chapters, things are not always what they seem. The best way to know what a person means is to ask them. We look at life through the lens of our experiences, which means sometimes we could be wrong. It is a known fact that different cultures interpret words and actions differently. Many cultures interpret body language, gestures, posture, and degree of eye contact differently.

For instance: In the U.S., we pretty much view the thumbs-up sign as a good thing, but in other countries like Iran, it is considered vulgar. If a person talks to us but does not look us in the eye, you would probably think that person was being sneaky and had something to hide. However, in some countries, not looking a person directly in the eye is considered respectful.

Misunderstandings Across Cultures

The list can go on and on, but in these two examples, you can see how one culture could get offended or offend another simply by doing what is normal or by interpreting what the other is doing based on their culture and experience. Now imagine if they were able to communicate with each other and explain. "Hey, I did not mean anything negative by giving you the thumbs-up. I was just trying to say you did a good job." "Oh, okay, because where I come from, when you give a thumbs-up signal, that is a vulgar sign." "Oh wow, I did not know that. I will make sure I don't do that again." And just like that, the weapon of offense cannot be used to destroy a budding relationship.

It is easy to understand this principle when we are dealing with people from other countries and different cultures, but why is it so hard to grasp when we are dealing with our family, friends, neighbors, co-workers, etc.? You know why? We assume since we are dealing with people from our same country, they must have the same culture. But what if I told you they may be from the same country, city, state, or even family but could have a different culture?

Hurt as a Culture

Did you know hurt can be a culture? Abuse? Insecurity? Because they come from a different culture than you, you may have to take the time to communicate with them to see why they are behaving differently than you.

One definition of culture is — the behaviors and beliefs characteristic of a particular social, ethnic, or age group. There are some behaviors that people who have been abused display. There are some behaviors that people who suffer from rejection display. There are some behaviors people display that you would need a Ph.D. to understand.

Since many of us are not psychologists, I have found an easier way to try to understand why people do what they do and to let them know that I am hurt by something that they did or said to me. That way is to communicate.

Biblical Lessons on Communication

The Bible shows us the power of what can be accomplished with communication and what happens when we no longer communicate. This scripture is from Genesis 11:1-9. I highlighted some passages I want you to pay attention to:

"Now the whole world had one language and a common speech. As people moved eastward, they found a plain in Shinar and settled there. They said to each other, 'Come, let's make bricks and bake them thoroughly.' They used brick instead of stone, and tar for mortar. Then they said, 'Come, let us build ourselves a city, with a tower that reaches to the heavens, so that we may make a name for ourselves; otherwise, we will be scattered over the face of the whole earth.' But the Lord came down to see the city and the tower the people were building. The Lord said, 'If as one people speaking the same language they have begun to do this, then nothing they plan to do will be impossible for them. Come, let us go down and confuse their language so they will not understand each other.' So the Lord scattered them from there over all the earth, and they stopped building the city. That is why it was called Babel—because there the Lord confused the language of the whole world. From there the Lord scattered them over the face of the whole earth."

As you can see, the world had one language and they were able to communicate with one another. They came up with a plan to build. They got together and started. The problem was that what they were building was not of God and would not glorify God, so the Lord put a stop to that by doing one thing: He stopped their ability to communicate. As a result, they were unable to keep building, and pretty soon, they were scattered all over. In other words, their relationships and vision came to a death, a separation.

The Enemy's Tactic

We know the devil has nothing new up his sleeve. He saw how effective stopping communication between people worked when the Lord did it, so he tries to use the same tactic. When you are joined together with people and you have a common goal of building something that will glorify God, whether it is a marriage, a friendship, a ministry, a company, or even your life, you must be aware that the enemy is going to come to try to stop communication.

Notice what the Lord said about being able to speak the same language, in other words, being able to communicate: "The Lord said, 'If as one people speaking the same language they have begun to do this, then nothing they plan to do will be impossible for them.'"

So you see how powerful being able to communicate is! This means if you want to build and you are connected to people who want to build, if everyone is speaking the same language, nothing will be impossible to build. The spirit of offense comes to make us not want to communicate or to communicate incorrectly, which stops whatever we were trying to build.

Practical Steps in Communication

When we get offended, many times we just don't bother speaking to that person. Or we yell, scream, and say things to hurt them. We are not communicating effectively, and before long, the building stops, and we scatter from each other.

If you have gone through all of the principles I have discussed in this book and you found yourself not being able to move on, maybe you need to open your mouth, not to tell them off, but to communicate to better understand them and for you to be better understood.

Since I had to deal with so many offenses, especially early in my Christian walk, I learned how just not to take them. It takes a whole lot to really get me upset, but there have been times when I did take offense, and I had to be willing to go to the person to explain why I was upset with them. Many times, they did not even know they had done something to offend me.

Overcoming Assumptions

Assumptions can be deadly. We make a lot of assumptions about people and we base a lot of decisions on our assumptions, but what if we are wrong? We may assume that person should know they did or said something that offended us, and because they are skipping through life without a care in the world, we get more offended because they "act like they didn't do anything." Well, what if they sincerely did not know?

As I mentioned at the beginning of this chapter, you may be communicating from different cultures, and the universal signs are really not that universal. Jesus gives us instructions on how we should handle different offenses: "If your brother or sister sins against you, rebuke them; and if they repent, forgive them. Even if they sin against you seven times in a day and seven times come back to you saying 'I repent,' you must forgive them." (Luke 17:3-4)

Notice we must rebuke them. Rebuke means to express sharp, stern disapproval of. To put it simply, we must let them know we disapprove of what they did or said. We have to let them know they hurt or disappointed us. Once we do, it is up to them if they are going to take the next step in getting things right. I have found that those who really love and seek to please the Lord will do whatever it takes to right any wrong, even if they don't think they did anything wrong.

Acting on the Word of God

"Therefore, if you are offering your gift at the altar and there remember that your brother or sister has something against you, leave your gift there in front of the altar. First, go and be reconciled to them; then come and offer your gift." (Matthew 5:23-24)

There have been quite a few times the Lord has had me apologize to someone who had a problem with me, even though I did not knowingly offend them. When I first had to do it, I fought for a minute until finally I said, "Ok Lord, let your will be done!" Although I had not knowingly done something to hurt or offend them, they had a problem with me for a reason, and since I knew they had a problem, I had to be the one to get it right.

Have you ever tried to resist what the Lord was telling you to do and finally you just give in? I did not get a positive response just because I humbled myself and went to get it right. Believe it or not, some people even took my apology the wrong way! But what the Lord told me was, "Ayanna, stop worrying about their reaction. You just do what I tell you to do because I am preparing you for where I am taking you."

The Heart of a Peacemaker

The same goes for you. If you know someone has a problem with you, don't just sit around and let the devil's negative voice be louder than your positive voice. Do what the Word of God says and communicate. Go and get it right. It is sad how many people want to be used by God to do great things but aren't willing to do the little things that show the character of Christ.

I believe the Lord is raising up individuals who truly want the Word of God to be made manifest in their lives. They have committed their lives to doing whatever it takes to bring God glory. Those are going to be the ones the Lord is going to really use because they are His children and they have His character. They live what they preach.

The others are the ones who are not willing to let their flesh die (their own will, emotions, and the way they want things done). They will get to the Pearly Gates talking about, "Lord, Lord, I prayed and cast out demons in your name." and the Lord will say, "Depart from me I never knew you." (Matthew 7:22). The reason He didn't know them is because their character looks nothing like His.

"Blessed are the peacemakers, for they will be called Children of God." (Matthew 5:9)

A true child of God is a peacemaker, not a hell-raiser. A true Child of God is always looking for ways to bring peace instead of war. They seek peace even when they need to rebuke or tell someone how they have hurt them. They themselves are apologetic if someone tells them they have wronged or offended others. When you sincerely are trying to bring peace, the Lord will give you peace as well as instructions prior to you going to address an offense with someone.

Don't just take matters into your own hands. Pray and ask the Lord to give you the words to speak. Ask the Lord to be the interpreter for each of you so that you both will be able to articulate your thoughts and words correctly while being able to understand the thoughts and words of the other correctly.

Recap:

- **The Power of Communication:** Clear communication is a weapon that destroys the spirit of offense. It allows us to understand others and to be understood.

- **Misunderstandings Across Cultures:** Cultural differences, including those shaped by personal experiences like hurt or insecurity, can lead to offenses. Communicating bridges these differences.

- **The Enemy's Strategy:** Satan uses miscommunication to disrupt relationships and halt progress. Unity and shared understanding make building and achieving goals possible.

- **Practical Communication:** When offense arises, seek clarity rather than assuming intentions. Express hurt constructively and work toward reconciliation.

- **Biblical Examples of Communication:** Scripture emphasizes the importance of addressing offenses and reconciling with others as acts of obedience and preparation for God's purpose.

- **The Heart of a Peacemaker:** True children of God seek peace and embody Christ's character through humility, forgiveness, and effective communication.

Reflection Questions:

1. How often do you communicate your feelings or clarify misunderstandings when offended?

_____

_____

_____

2. Are there cultural or personal differences that might affect how you and others interpret actions or words?

_____

_____

_____

3. How can you ensure your communication reflects the heart of a peacemaker, as described in Matthew 5:9?

_____

_____

_____

4. Do you rely on assumptions in your relationships, or do you take the time to seek clarity?

_____

_____

_____

5. What steps can you take to prioritize reconciliation and unity in situations of conflict?

_____

_____

_____

Action Steps:

- **Pray Before Speaking:** Ask God for the right words and a spirit of understanding before addressing an offense.

- **Seek Reconciliation:** Follow Jesus's instruction in Matthew 5:23-24 to go and reconcile with those who have issues with you.

- **Embrace Humility:** Even if you don't feel at fault, take the first step in addressing conflicts with a heart of peace.

- **Avoid Assumptions:** When someone offends you, ask for clarification instead of jumping to conclusions.

- **Live as a Peacemaker:** Strive to bring peace in every situation, reflecting the character of Christ through your words and actions.

Communication is a God-given tool to bridge gaps, heal wounds, and build unity. Let your life reflect Christ's love and humility by seeking understanding, reconciling with others, and speaking truth in love. In doing so, you will glorify God and strengthen the relationships entrusted to you.

"Lord, teach me to communicate with grace, humility, and clarity. Help me to seek peace and unity in every interaction, reflecting Your love and character."

Spiritual Growth Through Offense

I cannot tell you how much I have spiritually grown since I learned how not to let the spirit of offense prosper in my life. I can truly say I am experiencing peace that surpasses all understanding.

There are still areas of my life where I could get offended, and there are people who still try to say or do things that could offend me. However, I can truly say, "Devil, please!" When I look at what the Lord is doing and what He is speaking, I refuse to allow those the enemy sends my way to cause me to miss God and all He desires to do in my life. I want to encourage you to take the same stance. No one is worth you walking outside the will of God. Don't take Satan's bait.

Lessons from Joseph's Story

One of the best examples of not allowing offenses to stop you is the story of Joseph. If you don't know the story, you should read it (Genesis 37-45), especially when you are having trouble with offenses coming at you.

Joseph was young, had a dream from God, and favor from his father. He did not ask for the dream or favor, yet he was despised and rejected by his own brothers because of his dream and favor. They even plotted to take his life. This illustrates how people can feel offended because of your gifts or because they think what God gave you is better than what they received.

Many of us can relate. The Lord has given us dreams, visions, and favor, and instead of those close to us rejoicing and being glad for us, they become jealous and despise us. Many have tried to spiritually kill us due to their jealousy. However, they sadly do not realize that the dreams and favor of God on our lives are not just for us but for everyone connected to us, including them!

Joseph's brothers sold him into slavery for 20 pieces of silver to the Ishmaelites, who eventually sold him to Potiphar. They put a price tag on his life without realizing how valuable and priceless he really was. Many of us have been sold out, taken advantage of, and used for someone else's gain. When we no longer seem useful or beneficial, they sell us out to someone else.

The Lord gave Joseph a dream that he was going to be great, yet here he was being sold for a couple of pieces of silver. The enemy loves to use offenses and the things people do to us to make us question our worth and the big dreams the Lord has given us. But when you refuse to be offended or to stamp yourself with the same price tag others have tried to place on you, you will find yourself elevated despite what people have done or said about you.

Divine Favor Despite Betrayal

The favor and love of his earthly father Israel could not, and the love and favor from his Heavenly Father did not, prevent him from being sold. There are going to be times when people can do nothing for us and times when it seems the Lord is allowing people to treat us terribly. But we must continue to hold on and trust God that where we are is not our final destination.

Although Joseph was sold out by his older brothers and although the Lord allowed it to happen, the Lord was with Joseph and caused him to prosper. When you accept whatever the Lord allows without taking offense, He will cause you to prosper no matter where you find yourself.

Joseph was raised up and promoted, which lasted only for a little while because Potiphar's house was not his final destination. Potiphar was blessed because he invested in Joseph, but his heart was not right toward him. Potiphar was only looking at the blessings he was receiving by being connected to Joseph, and that is why when the enemy used Potiphar's wife to lie on Joseph, Potiphar quickly believed it and had him thrown in jail.

Divine Connections in Low Places

Potiphar had Joseph thrown in jail, but the favor of the Lord was still with Joseph. It was in jail that he met the person who would connect him to the person who would change his life and fulfill the dream that the Lord had shown him all those years before.

When the Lord is with you and His favor is upon you, two things will happen: First, you will be blessed no matter what situation you are in, and second, He will establish divine connections even in your lowest points. This is why you cannot afford to take offense no matter what people do to you. Taking offense will cause you to take your eyes off God and what He is doing and either put them on yourself ("I am so hurt, I can never trust again") or on the other person. Either way, you will be unable to see what the Lord desires to show you.

The Fulfillment of God's Plan

At the appointed time, the Lord caused Pharaoh to have a dream that only Joseph was able to interpret. Pharaoh sent for Joseph and recognized the spirit of God that was in him. Keep your integrity no matter what it looks like right now, and the Lord will cause people of influence, position, and wealth to look for and send for you when you least expect it.

Pharaoh dressed him in a royal robe, gave him a royal ring, had him ride in the royal chariot, and even married the priest's daughter. These blessings were beyond what Joseph could have imagined, but they were not the total fulfillment of the dream. Before the fulfillment of the dream came to full manifestation, Joseph had two sons: Manasseh, which means "The Lord has caused me to forget all of my troubles," and Ephraim, which means "The Lord has caused me to be fruitful in the land of my suffering."

Despite everything Joseph went through—rejection, betrayal, and lies—he was still able to produce Manasseh and Ephraim. This is only possible when you refuse to get offended and keep your focus on God. The Lord turned what the enemy meant for evil into something good, not just for Joseph but for many.

Recap:

- **Spiritual Growth Through Offense:** Learning not to let offense take root in your life leads to unparalleled spiritual growth and peace.

- **Joseph's Story:** Joseph's journey—from rejection by his brothers to ultimate promotion in Egypt—teaches us to trust God's plan despite adversities.

- **Divine Favor in Adversity:** God's favor works even in our lowest moments, turning setbacks into setups for His purpose.

- **Forgiveness and Productivity:** Refusing offense allows us to forgive, remain productive, and focus on what God is doing, rather than dwelling on personal hurts.

- **Birth Manasseh and Ephraim:** Just as Joseph's sons symbolized forgetting troubles and being fruitful in adversity, we, too, can experience these blessings by maintaining our integrity and faith in God.

- **Keep Your Focus on God:** Taking offense shifts focus from God to ourselves or others, hindering us from seeing His divine plan and purpose.

Reflection Questions:

1. How has offense impacted your spiritual growth in the past? Have you allowed it to prosper, or have you overcome it with God's help?

_____

_____

_____

2. In what ways does Joseph's story resonate with your own experiences of betrayal, rejection, or adversity?

_____

_____

_____

3. Are there situations or people in your life where you need to release offense and trust God's plan?

_____

_____

_____

4. How can you focus on God's promises and purposes, even when circumstances seem unfair or painful?

_____

_____

_____

5. What steps can you take to "birth Manasseh and Ephraim" in your own life, letting go of past hurts and thriving in the midst of adversity?

_____

_____

_____

Action Steps:

- **Meditate on Joseph's Journey:** Read Genesis 37-45, asking God to reveal His lessons for your life through Joseph's story.

- **Reject Offense:** When faced with rejection, betrayal, or injustice, declare, "Devil, please! I refuse to be offended!"

- **Focus on Forgiveness:** Actively pray for those who have wronged you, asking God to bless and heal them.

- **Keep a Gratitude Journal:** Document the ways God has brought favor and blessings in difficult times, shifting your focus from pain to praise.

- **Claim God's Promises:** Memorize and declare scriptures like Genesis 50:20: "You intended to harm me, but God intended it for good to accomplish what is now being done, the saving of many lives."

- **Trust the Process:** Remember that what the enemy means for evil, God will use for good. Stay faithful and patient as His plan unfolds.

Offense is a tool the enemy uses to derail us, but when we refuse to take the bait, God turns it into a tool for our growth and His glory. Like Joseph, we can experience unimaginable blessings when we keep our focus on God and His purpose. Let every trial produce a testimony that magnifies His goodness.

"Lord, help me to see offenses as opportunities for growth. Teach me to trust You completely and to forgive as You have forgiven me. May I be fruitful even in the land of my suffering, reflecting Your grace and power in every situation."

I Am *Still* Not Offended

Victory over offense isn't just about avoiding hurt feelings—it's about spiritual growth and maturity. Once you've learned the lessons and passed the tests, offenses stop coming with the same intensity. That's how you know it's a spirit. When you no longer allow offense to settle in your heart, it loses its grip on you.

Does it still try? Of course. The enemy likes to knock on the same door, hoping you'll forget what you've learned. But when you're quick to recognize offense for what it is and shut it down, it comes around less often.

A Recent Test

I recently had an experience that tested this principle in a way I wasn't expecting. Someone the enemy frequently uses offended me unexpectedly, and I wasn't prepared. For a moment, I stumbled. My initial reaction was, *"How dare they!"* I felt completely justified in pulling away from certain obligations because of what this person had done.

But then the Holy Spirit gently reminded me, *"Ayanna, you're revising Devil, Please!—did you think you wouldn't get tested?"*

I realized I couldn't just ignore the situation, so I decided to address the person. However, when I approached them, I did so with the wrong heart. I wasn't seeking restoration; I was trying to make a point. My mindset was, *"I see what you're doing, and it won't work."*

Not surprisingly, that conversation didn't go well. But through that experience, God taught me an important lesson: Even when you're right, your heart must be right too. The goal in addressing offenses should always be restoration, not retaliation.

Handling Offense God's Way

Here's what I've learned from that experience and many others:

- **Check your heart before you respond:** Is your motive pure? Are you seeking to restore the relationship or to retaliate?

- **Pray before you speak:** Ask God if it's the right time to address the situation and what He wants you to say.

- **Focus on growth:** The enemy's goal is to test your resolve and see if you're still standing firm. Use these moments to show that you're still growing and learning.

- **Remember the bigger picture:** Your response to offense isn't just about you. It's an opportunity to glorify God and show others His love and grace.

Living Unoffendable

Being unoffendable doesn't mean offenses never come your way—it means you handle them differently. You recognize them quicker, recover faster, and remain focused on God's purpose.

So when offense tries to knock on your door, declare with boldness: *"Devil, please—I am still not offended!"*

Offense: A Test and a Tool

I want you to remember a vital truth: Offense isn't just a feeling. It's a test, a tool, and an opportunity. Each time offense comes your way, you have a choice to make: Will you let it destroy what God is building in your life? Or will you use it as a stepping stone to your next level of spiritual maturity?

As we close this journey together, I want to remind you that walking in victory over offense is not just about avoiding hurt—it's about embracing freedom. It's about standing firm in your identity in Christ, recognizing the enemy's tactics, and refusing to let anything derail the plans God has for your life. The road may not always be easy, but the rewards are eternal: peace that surpasses understanding, relationships restored, ministries birthed, and lives transformed through your testimony. So stand tall in the knowledge that you are not alone, you are growing, and you are equipped. With every offense that comes your way, let your response glorify God, strengthen your faith, and bring healing to others. Walk boldly in your freedom, declaring with unwavering confidence, "Devil, please—I am STILL not offended!"

Closing Prayer

Heavenly Father,

We come before You with grateful hearts, humbled by the truth and wisdom You have revealed throughout this journey. Thank You for reminding us that offense is not the end of the story, but an opportunity for growth, healing, and deeper intimacy with You.

Lord, we acknowledge that in our own strength, we fall short. We confess the times we've allowed offense to take root in our hearts, hindering our relationships and our walk with You. But today, we choose freedom. We choose to release every hurt, every grudge, and every wound into Your capable hands.

Father, teach us to see others through Your eyes—eyes of compassion, grace, and unconditional love. Help us to walk in humility, recognizing our own imperfections and extending the same mercy and forgiveness You so freely give to us. Strengthen us to resist the schemes of the enemy, who seeks to divide and destroy. Empower us by Your Spirit to rise above every offense and reflect Your light in the midst of darkness.

Lord, we declare that the enemy has no hold on us. Offense will not define us; Your love will. Bitterness will not consume us; Your joy will. Division will not prevail; Your peace will. We claim the victory You have already secured for us through Jesus Christ, and we walk forward in that freedom with confidence and boldness.

As we close this book, may the lessons we've learned take root in our hearts and bear fruit in our lives. May we live as ambassadors of Your grace, examples of Your forgiveness, and vessels of Your transformative power. Use us, Lord, to draw others to You, that they may also experience the freedom that comes from living unoffended.

Thank You, Father, for Your unending love, Your unshakable truth, and Your unfailing promises. We trust You, we honor You, and we give You all the glory.

In Jesus' name,
Amen.

About Ayanna

Ayanna Lynnay is a visionary author, speaker, and mentor dedicated to inspiring others to step boldly into their God-given purpose. As the founder of ChosenButterfly Publishing, Ayanna has helped countless authors bring their stories to life, with many achieving #1 Amazon bestseller status. Through her publishing company and writing courses, she equips aspiring writers with practical tools and faith-based encouragement, empowering them to share their stories with confidence.

Ayanna is the author of *Devil, Please I Am Still Not Offended*, a transformative book addressing the damaging effects of offense while equipping readers to overcome its grip. Her devotional, *Seasons Do Change*, offers spiritual encouragement for navigating life's transitions, and her book *Destined to Dream: Equipped and Graced to Overcome* explores the power of faith, resilience, and purpose in pursuing God-given dreams. She has also contributed her voice to numerous compilation books on topics such as divorce, starting over, faith, and purpose, adding depth and insight to a wide range of discussions. In her writing courses, Ayanna integrates the use of AI tools to make storytelling more accessible and impactful for writers at every level.

Ayanna serves as an Elder in her local church, Tabernacle of Praise Buffalo, under the leadership of Pastor Charles McCarley. Her commitment to ministry reflects her passion for helping others grow in their faith and walk in alignment with God's purpose for their lives.

In addition to her professional and ministry work, Ayanna is the proud mother of two incredible daughters, Shakiya and Lauriyana, who inspire her daily with their strength and creativity.

With a heart deeply rooted in faith, Ayanna is passionate about helping others recognize their potential, trust God through challenges, and embrace the dreams He has placed in their hearts. Her message is clear: the Lord is able to transform your life into a blessed life you never knew existed when you love and serve Him.

When she's not writing, teaching, or ministering, Ayanna enjoys creating courses, mentoring, and developing programs that nurture both spiritual and professional growth. Her vibrant personality, unwavering faith, and commitment to excellence leave a lasting impact on everyone she encounters. Ayanna's journey is a testament to the power of faith, perseverance, and God's ability to turn every step—even missteps—into a testimony for His glory. Her life and work are dedicated to helping others realize their dreams and live lives transformed by the power of God.

If you would like to take the accompanying course for this book, seek mentorship, or explore other courses designed to help you grow into who God desires you to be, visit **www.transformation-station.org**.

N nIf you aspire to become a published author or are an aspiring writer looking for expert guidance, visit **https://courses.chosenbutterflypublishing.com** Through her courses and services, Ayanna Lynnay and her team are dedicated to equipping writers with the tools, strategies, and support they need to bring their stories to life and make a lasting impact.